About the

Jack Dawes is a retired teacher, having spent forty-two years at the chalk face in a number of establishments across the country. He has experienced teaching at the sharp end in the State sector and also at the other end in the independent sector. He has taught science and computing (mainly) to children whose ages range from 4 years to 19 years, but has also covered lessons in virtually every other subject – Languages, Art, Drama, Maths, Design & Technology, English, Classics, History and R.E.

As a retiree, Jack enjoys working on his allotment and his garden. For many years he enjoyed cycling, but this is diminishing as the traffic grows on the roads and he is not a young man any more. Walking appears to be the way forward. He has developed an appreciation of good wine after many years of practise and also enjoys a glass or three of real ale from time to time. Holidays abroad are an important part of his retirement, especially in the sun, where he can spend time walking and visiting the many beautiful areas on this planet.

He has been blessed with two daughters and two grandchildren, with whom he corresponds with regularly, but only occasionally visits because of the large distances involved.

Jack lives in Stamford with his wife who goes into town shopping on a Saturday afternoon, while he watches the footy on the television …

I would like to dedicate the book to my two daughters, Helen and Hannah, who had to put up with my antics for many years.

To my good friends Joy & Val. I hope you enjoy this 'intellectual tome'!

Peter

(AKA Jack Dawes)

Jack Dawes

MEMORIES ARE MADE OF THESE

AUSTIN MACAULEY
PUBLISHERS LTD.

Copyright © Jack Dawes (2017)

The right of Jack Dawes to be identified as author of this work has been asserted by him in accordance with section 77 and 78 of the Copyright, Designs and Patents Act 1988.

All rights reserved. No part of this publication may be reproduced, stored in a retrieval system, or transmitted in any form or by any means, electronic, mechanical, photocopying, recording, or otherwise, without the prior permission of the publishers.

Any person who commits any unauthorized act in relation to this publication may be liable to criminal prosecution and civil claims for damages.

A CIP catalogue record for this title is available from the British Library.

ISBN 9781786934543 (Paperback)
ISBN 9781786934550 (E-Book)
www.austinmacauley.com

First Published (2017)
Austin Macauley Publishers Ltd.
25 Canada Square
Canary Wharf
London
E14 5LQ

Introduction

"People have an annoying habit of remembering things they shouldn't."

Christopher Paolini, Eragon

How is it I can remember things that happened over sixty years ago and yet, I cannot remember things that happened yesterday? Are the events more notable from a long time ago? Maybe if I lived for another sixty years or so, I will remember what happened yesterday but then they too will be memories of over sixty years of age.

Just before I retired from teaching, I was asked to cover a Year 9 Latin lesson for an absent Classics teacher. Thankfully, I had been given instructions as to what the class had to do and as I looked down the class list, I noticed that they seemed quite a bright lot. As the lesson got underway, I explained that it was a long time since I had done Latin (over fifty years), but if there was a problem, I would certainly try to help. Surprise, surprise! The lesson was about five minutes old, when a couple of the kids had a problem with vocabulary and another had a problem with grammar.

I was amazed, as from nowhere both of the answers sprang into my head. Furthermore, I seemed to conjure up the answers for most of the other problems that surfaced. How all of this happened, I had no idea. I couldn't remember what I had had for breakfast that morning. Nor could I remember driving to work. What was the stimulus that made me remember all of the Latin vocabulary and grammar?

I then started thinking about events that occurred earlier in my life and I was amazed to find that the majority of them were easy to remember, even incredible details, smells, tastes etc were forthcoming. I thought I had better jot a few things down as later on I might forget them, and then some of the riotous events that occurred would be lost forever.

Chapter 1

Schooldays

Coup d'etat

It is always amazing how lavatorial humour brings out the animal in the adolescent male. So it was with the incident involving the farting machines.

It was standard issue at school to have a blue hymn book with a hard back, which fitted snugly into a blazer pocket. It was brought out every morning but only used when the need arose, such as a Master mingling with the rabble. However, an ingenious use was found for the blue, hard backed Ancient and Modern – the farting machine.

A farting machine consisted of a knitting needle bent in the shape of a U, with a piece of elastic stretched across the ends and a button attached to the centre. This could then be wound many times to produce a very tense piece of elastic, ready to uncoil itself vigorously at the first available opportunity. Of course, on its own, it was relatively harmless, but combined with the hardbacked Ancient and Modern and released in the pocket, it became a formidable weapon capable of reducing a grown man to tears.

As was the custom in School assembly, a prefect always read the lesson or said the Lord's Prayer to the rest of the School. So it was, on this one day when word spread around like wildfire that "Pud", the most hated prefect in school was to say the Lord's Prayer. All of the fourth and fifth form (now called Year 10 and 11), immediately began to arm their machines, slowly winding the buttons during registration. Every bit of hate they had mustered over the years for this one prefect was carefully entwined in thick elastic. Madame Desfarges at the guillotine was an amateur compared to this.

Finally, the bell for assembly sounded and last minute checks on the tension of the elastic were made. The School made its way to the Great Hall for the solemn occasion. Quite a number of boys were noted entering the hall clutching their pockets. However, few Masters realised that secret weapons had been primed and the hands on the pockets were the safety catches to prevent premature ejaculation.

There was a definite air of expectancy, as the hymn was sung with more than three times the usual volume. This indeed was a very special occasion. Silence prevailed as the Headmaster announced the Lord's Prayer. Gone were the bronchial attacks. Gone were the shuffling feet and the itchy bottoms. The silence was deafening as the immortal words were uttered...

"Our Father, which art in Heaven," as 120 farting machines was released.

Fait accompli.

Brainwaves

It has been said that a little knowledge is a dangerous thing. It couldn't have been proved much more convincingly than in our experiments with brainwaves.

We often spent lunchtime in the sixth form hanging around in the science labs. It was very convenient for those who wanted to do extra work or just get away from the junior plebs. Quite often these gatherings led to frantic discussions and debate, strangely enough, about scientific matters. It was long before the science labs remained locked, although this incident probably had something to do with labs being locked over the lunch break.

One lunch break started the same as many others. Someone had heard or read that brainwaves were transmitted at x cycles per second. The reasoned discussion that followed led to the assumption that if brainwaves travelled at this speed, then if another wave at the same frequency was transmitted at a time when the brainwave was at a peak and the alternate wave was at a trough, then one would cancel out the other. Something like ripples in a pond from two equal and opposite sources. How could we prove this? We would need some human guinea pigs. Where could we get these 'volunteers'? It would be difficult to press gang some of the lower school into doing this, especially when we did not know what would happen.

Someone had a brilliant idea! Just below the physics lab was a small quadrangle where the first year (Year 7) played football with a tennis ball. It was fairly secluded and only overlooked by the physics lab and a ground floor glass corridor where the prefects used to hang out. They could be our guinea pigs and they would not know anything was happening.

Everyone set to, to gather the equipment. A frequency modulator was obtained, along with a massive amplifier and two large speakers. Protective headphones were to be worn by the team of experimenters. The equipment was quickly connected and the speakers were situated by an open window pointing down into the quad. Headphones were on, the frequency modulator was set at the correct frequency and everything was ready for the big switch on.

What happened next beggar's belief?

As the switch was thrown, twenty young footballers fell to the ground as one! As this was seen by the physics lab crew, the switch was immediately turned back off. The panic that ensued was incredible. Windows slammed shut. Headphones removed. Equipment dismantled and stashed away at the speed of light then, stunned silence. The prefects in the glass corridor ran out to the scene of devastation and one was despatched to the staff room for assistance. Members of staff arrived on the scene to administer first aid to the unconscious youngsters. Some appeared to 'come round', but were extremely woozy! After a few minutes, five ambulances appeared in the school playground and the semi-conscious footballers were stretchered in. By this time, word had got around school that a major disaster had struck the first year and a large crowd had gathered, which made it quite difficult for the medics and ambulances to carry on. Soon, all of the injured were in the ambulances and were then ferried away.

Upstairs in the physics lab, the atmosphere was also very, very tense. What had they done? A very sheepish group of scientists prepared for the recriminations and were extremely quiet in afternoon lessons, something that made the teachers even more edgy. Minutes passed without the Headmaster and/or the police bursting in to make arrests for GBH or even worse. The minutes turned to hours and last, it was home time. It was with great relief that about a dozen sixth formers, still trembling with trepidation, made their way homeward. Not much had been said between them, just a combined fear that they had done something extremely dangerous, if not illegal.

The following morning loomed and the only topic of conversation was the headlines in the local Echo that evening:-

"MYSTERY VIRUS STRIKES SCHOOLCHILDREN"

This was coupled with a full page front spread of the incident and also much discussion from doctors, teachers and parents on the inside pages. Most of the children were released from hospital after observation and only one remained, due to a severe asthma attack.

Had the physicists got away without charges being laid? The school was in a very sombre mood and no 'farting machines' were released during assembly that morning. Prayers were said and the injured were given two days off school and a weekend to recover. The physicists vowed never to do anything like that again and did everyone learn from this incident? I don't think so... Enter the chemists!

Substance X

After the incident in the physics lab, school returned to its normal stable state. Only a few misdemeanours were reported. There were the usual activities of the school bully and the school liar, mainly concerned with extorting goodies from the young kids in exchange for protection. The school tuck shop never seemed to make a profit, although it seemed in constant use. The sixth form 'looked after' the tuck shop and made sure it never made a loss. If it did, it would raise suspicions from the staff and could be the cause of drastic measures to monitor the takings and check the flow of stock. School life became rather boring until the chemists added a little spice to the proceedings after various lunchtime experiments. While the chemistry teacher was having his customary tipple in the stock room, the sixth form made an amazing discovery. If some household crystals were added to ammonia solution and left to almost dry out, the mixture could be spread around the floor and after drying completely, became almost invisible. Then, when it was walked over, the slightest amount of friction caused a small explosion. This was just what the school needed at the moment, as it was still reeling from the physics lunchtime experiment. A production line was set up and a large quantity of this Substance X was spread over the floor and around the teacher's desk. The perpetrators then sat still and waited for the bell at the start of the afternoon lesson.

The door was flung open on the bell and the school swots poured in on time. The look of surprise over their horn rimmed specs was spectacular, as one by one they were greeted with exploding feet – theirs! The noise was quite alarming. So much in fact that the chemistry teacher left his beverage and rolled out of the stock room to discover what the commotion was all about. He was quite surprised too, to find that not only did his feet explode, but when he put his hands on his bench to steady himself, they exploded too. As he ran out of the room to press the fire alarm on the outside wall, he may have been surprised that his path exploded all the way to the door. Meanwhile, the swots were screaming and wailing as though they had been hit by a salvo of gunfire. Then the fire alarm went off. Everyone piled out of the room (some exploding on the way) and assembled in the playground just as it started to pour with rain. Registers could not be taken as it was so wet, so everyone was re-routed to the sports hall.

After the registers were taken and no-one had appeared to be dead, the chemistry teacher tried to explain to the Headmaster what had occurred. I'm sure he must have noticed the alcohol on his breath and the slurred speech, coupled with the fact that the Head was a classics graduate and hadn't a clue what Mr. Chemistry was burbling about. After a lengthy discourse, we were finally dismissed and marched back to our classrooms, where we discovered the lovely Iris (lab technician) had already cleaned up. Our teacher was in no fit state to teach us and departed to the inner sanctum, where he no doubt poured himself a stiff one. We read a book on organic chemistry for the last twenty minutes of the lesson, having enjoyed ourselves immensely.

Because the Headmaster had threatened to publicly humiliate the person or persons responsible for this latest debacle, we decided to lay low for a while until someone thought up another brilliant wheeze. We didn't wait too long before coming up with another master plan.

One of the teaching blocks was a building four storeys high and on each landing was a set of boys and girls toilets. They were next door to each other and were used frequently after each lesson. It was a constant source of amazement to the boys as the crashing of toilet seats and girly giggles emanated from the girls' toilets at the various breaks. The boys, on the other hand, contented themselves with seeing who could pee the highest up the tiled wall. This would be the starting point for our latest escapade.

During one of our chemistry lessons when the teacher had done pages and pages of theory, he retired early to the inner sanctum for refreshment and left us to finish off some basic experiments and do some book work. This was what we had been waiting for, as we knew he would not reappear before the end of the lesson. We set to and made some Substance X sludge and put it in a beaker for later. Towards the end of the lesson, we all packed up and disappeared before the bell. We legged it towards the classroom block and painted the Substance X on the girls' toilet seats and popped next door to the boys' toilets to await the bell for break.

As the bell rang, we were trembling with excitement and trepidation as the girly laughter and chit chat echoed around the toilets. The seats crashed down and the silence was momentary. The first bang was quickly followed by the second, third and fourth and was temporarily drowned out by the screams. Imagine how thrilled the girls were when they rushed out of the toilets with their knickers round their ankles. Even more thrilling were the two lines of sixth formers forming a tunnel, each holding a placard with "7.6", "8.4", "5.2" etc.

We nearly got expelled for that but luckily, the girls in their panic, didn't recognise any of us and so the Headmaster could only issue the whole year with a verbal warning!

Dogfish

In the days before Sir Keith Joseph, Kenneth Baker et al, it was customary in schools to have respect for teachers and indeed pay them a living wage. They were occasionally feared, but generally were highly respected by pupils, parents and the general public. It was the case too that when teachers took lessons for absent colleagues, they did so with grace, knowing that there might be a time when someone would have to stand in for them.

Whilst in the sixth form, it was necessary for our biology teacher, who was also Deputy Head, to stand in for the Headmaster who had to retire suddenly because of ill health. Now it became our lot to cope on many occasions without a teacher for about a term, whilst a new Head Teacher was appointed. It was assumed that because we were in the sixth form, we were responsible adults and we were to show our maturity by attempting A Level biology from a text book and practising dissection without any supervision whatsoever. How wrong they were!

Naturally enough, the topic of conversation moved on to include football and other sports and that was the springboard for a new sport which was so exciting, it could even be offered television rights. Here started "Dogfish Bombing". Even now, after all of these years, the name still sends a tingle somewhere or other.

It was found by lengthy experiment, that if a dogfish is cut on the lateral surface and part of the skin removed, it will stick on the ceiling with a slurping sound (when thrown length ways) and stay there for quite a while. After many further experiments, it was discovered that the length of time it stayed on the ceiling was directly proportional to the weight of the fish. In fact large graphs were drawn to prove this was the case. However, whilst heavily involved in this proof, we ran out of dogfish. Immediately, an SOS went to the acting Headmaster, who gave us a blank requisition form and one hundred and twenty dogfish were immediately ordered.

When these new dogfish arrived in four huge boxes, the acting Headmaster was very impressed, thinking that we were working like fury and ploughing our way through the syllabus. However, he was less impressed later on when he received the invoice for the dogfish.

A great Friday afternoon was planned with one hundred and twenty-three dogfish to carefully weigh, dissect and stick on the ceiling and time how long they were to remain there. The project got an unexpected boost, when a maths teacher was taken ill and some of the maths class came to join us. They were not all as stuffy as we had expected and quickly joined in the spirit of the thing, by organising a "book" on various ugly looking dogfish. Clocks were primed. Charts were drawn. Tables were laid out. A production line followed, with dissectors, instrument providers and finally ceiling stickers all doing their bit for science.

Imagine the sheer horror and panic that ensued when in walked the acting Headmaster. At first he was not noticed, as everyone was working harder than they had ever done in a lesson. Then his dulcet tones rang out

"Is everything alright? You seem to be working very well."

On hearing this, the room became engulfed in silent prayer.

"Please God/Allah/Vishnu/Buddha/Kali et al, don't let him look up!"

The silence was certainly ecclesiastical as hands were clasped under the desk in homage to the aforesaid deities, with the rest of the class doing a brilliant imitation of dogfish dissection.

"Is there anything I can do while I'm here?"

"Oh no sir," said the school liar, "we are getting on just fine."

"Please don't look up. Please don't look up. Please don't look up."

A silent Buddhist chant was roaring from the minds of the assembled throng. The chant suddenly changed.

"Please bugger off. Please bugger off. Please bugger off."

"Well, if you're sure there's nothing you want me to do."

The silent chant reached a crescendo.

"Please bugger off. Please bugger off. Please bugger off."

"I've got some paperwork to attend to. Carry on!"

The door closed with a clunk behind him and within five seconds, the first of the hundred or so timed dogfish fell off the ceiling!

Sam Spelk and other animals

One of our 'favourite' teachers was a physics teacher to whom we gave the nickname "Sam Spelk". Poor Sam. He was about four feet ten inches tall and six and a half stone soaking wet. He was about as strong as a drink of water. To cap it all, he had a rather unfortunate appearance too; black greasy hair hanging down halfway across his brow, very similar to Hitler, and huge black glasses perched on the end of his nose like Hank Marvin of the Shadows or Joe Ninety! Couple this lot with his super acne, and you definitely have a candidate for everyone to kick sand in his face.

Poor Sam! He was obviously a brilliant mathematician and physician, but he could not teach for toffee. He was as welcome in schools as a skunk in a perfumery. Why he ever decided to teach and whoever passed this guy on his teaching practice, I will never know. From the moment he entered the room and dropped all of his books and papers on the floor, we knew it was our mission to show Sam that teaching was not for him, even if this meant very naïve and subtle forms of explanation.

During the first five minutes of the very first lesson, we were all lost. Even those doing advanced maths had no idea what all the formulae meant. To make matters worse, like all good scientists, he had appalling handwriting. When we tried to interject and explain the fact that we hadn't a clue what he was talking about, there was no stopping him. Detailed formulae and equations were still pouring forth from his mouth and his hand was fervently trying to cope with all that his addled brain could pour out, leaving a mass of hieroglyphics on the blackboard. It was as if he was on automatic pilot! How could we attract his attention?

We were very fortunate to have in our class, not only the school liar, but also the school pyromaniac, who had obtained his full colours for burning down the school technical drawing department. He was also made Captain of the School Fire Raising Team as he set fire to the fire engine that came to put out the fire in the technical drawing department. As usual, he was playing with matches and flamethrowers under the desk whilst Sam was rambling on.

Just for a laugh, someone turned on the gas taps at the centre of the bench. These were in groups of four and they burst into flames of about a metre high. Sam pretended not to notice and so the next bench miraculously did the same. Even then he continued to ignore the flames and continued with his 'physicobabble'. So, to draw attention fully to our needs, all of the gas taps were turned on and set alight. This looked even more spectacular with the blinds down. With the size of the flames, it was impossible to get to the gas taps to turn them off and Sam, at last, stopped his burblings to listen to what we had to say. We tried to explain to him that we could not understand what he was talking about, but he seemed to get very irate and upset and kept shouting,

"Turn them off! Turn them off!" or something along those lines.

After we had doused the flames, which had engulfed Sam's leather patches on the elbows of his jacket, he began jabbering hysterically about job satisfaction and lack of money in the teaching profession. Why had he not taken his father's advice to become a Methodist minister and how was he going to sew new patches on his jacket.

This was only the beginning. Poor Sam! Things deteriorated rapidly after this. When we wanted to attract his attention next, it was not a case of raising the hand and waiting to be noticed. Oh no. We would have waited forever and a day. More subtle means were used, such as ball bearings on the floor, paper aeroplanes, rubber bungs bouncing off the teacher's desk and even bits of half dissected rats hitting the blackboard. When the first dart was thrown, that was when I knew I was not going to pass A level physics. It may have been obvious from this last saga that poor Sam was not at all respected as a teacher. We had tried our best to indicate to him that he should not have become a teacher; teaching was not his strong point. However, it was some twenty-one years later that I learned from someone, who I met at a meeting, that Sam was not only alive and well, but indeed still thriving on the garbage dished out by all of his pupils. I also learned that he had changed schools twenty-six times and never had a nervous breakdown. Now if that isn't sheer stupidity/stamina, I don't know what is. Some teachers never learn!

PE and games

Just as Sam was the least respected member of staff, Bob Bailey was the most respected. Bob was the PE teacher and he was revered by all. He had been and still was a brilliant gymnast. He also must have been a very good looking guy in his time, the George Clooney of his era, but not quite as smooth! He had great bearing and stature, which was all the more admirable as he had a wife who suffered from multiple sclerosis and this in itself must have been heart rending. Yet he never shirked from his duty, never felt sorry for himself and gave great words of wisdom to anyone who had problems.

One of his favourite lessons was to send everyone out on a cross country run, giving them a ten minute start before following up on his bike, complete with his trusty 'cudgel'. Anyone he overtook got a whack on the backside with this 'cudgel' and got another one as they arrived in the door of the gym changing room. His trusty 'cudgel' was a sawn off cricket bat the blade had been sawn off to leave about 20cms. It was indeed a fearsome weapon and it was wielded with some force. (Rumour had it he called the bat Torfreda, which was the name of Hereward the Wake's wife. Maybe this had some significance, but no-one knew the reason why).

Anyhow, Bob always used to whack the kids with a smile on his face. (I later learned that one could get away with all sorts of misdemeanours, provided there was a smile on the face). Our crowd only once got the bat, whereas the majority of the year had this pleasure two or three times a week! The reason for this was that as soon as we were let out of the door on our weekly cross country, most of our companions took off across the field and went out into the countryside. We, on the other hand, ran in the opposite direction across another field, over a fence and into our friends' house, where we spent a pleasant hour drinking coffee and listening to records. When we saw the first boy reappear across the field, we quickly vacated the premises, splashed a little mud in all the right places and off we went, long before the arrival of the cudgel.

This happened very regularly, until disaster struck! We all got picked for the Schools' cross country team to compete in the inter schools cross country championships. This was indeed a time to panic! None of us had run further than the local chip shop and there was no getting out of this without a doctor's note. That week, the local surgery was inundated with petty illness. Everything from brucellosis to gangrene was suspected, but to no avail. Only one note was issued and that was for athlete's foot. What a laugh! There wasn't an athlete amongst us. All of that eating soil and hitting toes with hammers had not worked. We had to accept our fate

The day of the cross country arrived, a perfect day. Blue sky with a few clouds, cool with just a little breeze. Our School team consisted of the School number one, the School liar, the School pyromaniac, the School's largest tool, the School bully and seven other pathetic specimens. What a shambolic group! We had all been issued with new vests and Bob Bailey had given us a team talk about what tactics to use, and how we should stick together until the last mile and then make a break for the finish. This was really scary. How could we come out of this with only a small amount of egg on our faces?

Just about the only redeeming feature in our team was that we had the School bully. He proved very useful in the changing rooms before the race, threatening some of the smaller runners with a dandruff salad if they overtook any of our team. But even this could not save us from utter humiliation. As the race started, we stuck together, just as Bob Bailey had instructed. This was very difficult for the School number one runner, who would have been walking if he had gone any slower. It must have been quite amusing too as there was this large group of runners/walkers who would not overtake the School bully for fear of being decked. Then a flash of inspiration

As we approached the second bend, which was near a wood, I noticed there was a huge puddle of water and an arrow directing the runners along a fairly narrow path along the side. A quick sprint by the School number one around the bend was needed to uproot the arrow and direct it through the enormous puddle/lake. This was successfully achieved by a lot of sheltering to block the view, not to mention the fake heart attack/epileptic fit by the School liar.

Now this tactic in itself was not exactly a world shattering event, but it did slow up the opposition sufficiently. Coupled with the School bully's threats, we came an incredible 16th place out of 40 schools. This did not please Bob Bailey very much as we were runners up the previous year and he was mighty suspicious. So much so, that on our next cross country run, he did not wait the usual ten minutes before setting off on his bike, but rather set off after two minutes and quickly caught the School number one. There was no sight or sound of our mob as we had disappeared almost at once and were busily drinking coffee and listening to Jimi Hendrix and the like. The euphoria was not to last as Bob Bailey was waiting for us on our return, Torfreda in hand

English

Some of our teachers were quite bizarre and nerdy. Many had odd characteristics like chewing their wrist whilst sitting down, strange coughing sounds almost like Tourettes and many other habits.

One teacher in particular, Joe Stead, had the most ridiculous routine which he did every morning. On his arrival in a beat up old Ford, he would park normally at the front of the school and then get out after collecting his briefcase from the front seat. Here began his 'ritual'. He would look like he was walking to the door, when he would turn suddenly as though he had forgotten something and stare at his motor for about thirty seconds. He would then walk back to his Ford and examine closely all four tyres, bending right down to do so. He would then stand up, take a few paces back, look at the tyres and then begin the examination once again. On special days, he would even try and feel the tyre pressure with his fingers! He would then walk away towards the door, stop and 'admire' his handiwork for a good few seconds. Just exactly what he was trying to do and what was going through his brain at the time, no-one knows. This ritual was repeated in exact detail every morning.

Naturally, as keen eyed young hooligans, we quickly latched on to this and tried to distract him from an upstairs window. This gentleman was not for turning. He ignored the knocks on the windows, the boyish laughter, the paper aeroplanes and the contents of various litter bins raining down. His routine could not be stopped. We therefore did the only thing left in our armoury, which was to write a song about it or more correctly write lyrics to an existing tune from the TV programme 'The Beverley Hill-Billies' and the lyrics went like this:-

The Ballad of Joe Stead
(To the tune of the Beverley Hillbillies)

Come and listen to my story 'bout a man named Joe Stead.
A poor English teacher, barely kept his tyres tread.
And then one day he was looking at his tyre
And somebody said, "There's a hole a little higher!"
Puncture that is, black hole, Texas tread
Well the next thing you know old Joe's a millionaire.
His kin folk said, "Get some new tyres on there."
They said, "The West Midlands is the place to be."
So he loaded up his kit and he moved to Coventry.
City that is. Rubber tyres, moving cars...

Art

Art was not really a strong point on the curriculum, as the art room was the domain of the "nutter". It was stuck out on a limb, separated from the rest of the school by a corridor containing various objet d'art, which looked like enormous Jim Henson creations. The corridor got very little light and the sheer size of these creations (which were actually papier mache Vikings and Anglo Saxons holding battle axes and swords), made the whole place quite eerie. None of the first years (Year 7) liked going into the art corridor and there was a rumour that the ghost of a previous art teacher walked the corridor. Everyone who entered the art corridor and department did so very quietly. Not only was it spooky, but every now and then the "nutter" used to melt through the walls and shock people.

Now the "nutter" was the recognised art teacher. An enormous man, about six feet six inches tall and very thin which made him look even taller, especially as he wore his trousers 'half mast'. His huge Jewish looking nose had been broken at some time and was at about 45° to the rest of his face. He wore some of the most amazing combinations of clothes I have ever seen. Things like purple shirts with a green tie and a red V neck jumper were coupled with blue trousers and brown leather sandals. The handbag was the icing on the cake. No-one dared to ridicule him, as he was likely to explode at any time. A very impatient man at the best of times, he certainly was a Bohemian in the true sense of the word.

It was his task to try and teach us the finer points of still life drawing and to a budding group of scientists, this was no easy task. Firstly, he gave us an entirely free hand. Draw anything that sprang to mind. As we had not yet discovered girls and booze and other adolescent distractions, we set about drawing mainly spaceships and submarines. Some of our drawings were very good, but not quite the still life he had imagined.

However, we persevered and listened carefully to his words of wisdom regarding perspective, and our spaceships and submarines improved in leaps and bounds. He began to feel that we hadn't quite got the hang of that, so he introduced some objects from around the class. This consisted of a table and a chair in a corner of a room and we huddled round with our drawing boards and paper holders. It was quite remarkable how much better these looked with a few ray guns and periscopes. Even when the standard bowl of plastic fruit was introduced, a banana looks very much like a spaceship! With a little imagination, the stalk on an apple makes an amazing periscope. It was during the final still life of rockets launching from an undersea base (wine bottles and glasses), that the "nutter" finally flipped. He picked up the wine bottles and threw them across the room, demolishing a semi finished enormous papier mache muppet and banished us forever from his art room. It was not until many years later that I realised we were probably the finest collection of spaceship and submarine artists in the country.

Science

Our chemistry teacher, who had hit the bottle in a big way, was having an affair with the wife of the geography teacher. This was blatantly obvious to everyone except the geography teacher, who was so wrapped up in his subject he did not notice what was going on around him. Not only was he having an affair, but he frequently had do's with the lab technician whose name was Iris, and she was a right little flower. Many were the times that the meths bottle was broached and the raucous goings on went on. Whether or not the lab technician was broached was a constant topic of debate.

It was after one of his infamous binges that he announced we were to have a trip out of school to see something scientific. Could it be that we were to visit Calder Hall (now called Sellafield), a nuclear power station? Or even the local ICI works? Or even a blast furnace? No. We were going to visit the local brewery for educational reasons of course. Brilliant! Only our chemistry teacher could come up with this. This visit was obviously essential for us to get good grades at A level. The date had been set. No time for complaints, the minibus had been booked and away we were to go. However, there were twenty in the group and the minibus held sixteen. No problem. Our chemistry teacher was to take his car!

So off we went, four of us in his car, which was a 3 litre beast and at the time was a little speedy. We covered the journey from school to the brewery in twenty minutes, the minibus took an hour. We wondered just how much he had to drink before he set off. We pulled into the car park and were ushered into a sumptuous lounge, whereupon we were offered the hospitality of the house. Anything we wanted we could have. Well, I've heard of Nirvana, but this was ridiculous. After a couple of beers, the minibus arrived with the rest of the group and the tour began. The guide was very impressed with the biochemical questions we asked. So much so that he asked us to stay for lunch and discussed careers in the brewing industry with us. The School bully had previously been round and ordered the 'swots' to keep this bloke talking while the rest of us continued drinking.

Our teacher too sank rather a lot of neck oil and by the time we said our 'thank you' and 'goodbyes', he was well and truly elephants' trunk. As we clambered into his car, we remembered the fast and furious inward journey. Now this guy was more than a little the worse for wear. As we screamed out of the car park and round the first bend, the first window was opened for the first of many encounters with Hughie and Ralph. The teacher was not going to stop or slow down and the constant violent motion of the car had caused havoc with the eight pints of ale and the pork pie salad we had for lunch. It must have been an amazing sight as we pulled in to the school car park at sixty miles an hour, with all the windows open and four white faced sixth formers hanging out and puking all down the sides. For this and other episodes, we were awarded our full school colours in alcohol abuse.

School Trips

We loved going away on 'school outings'. Some of these were just for the day, whilst others were for longer periods. One of our teachers, Ralph Bridgewater, was a fanatical football fan and supported the local team which was then in the second tier of English football, known as Division 2. It was a good system, because the top division was known as Division 1 and the third tier was Division 3, as well as the fourth tier being Division 4. Life was not complicated back then!

Our local team had progressed very well in the FA Cup but unfortunately were drawn against Manchester United at Old Trafford. This was a daunting challenge as United were at the top of Division 1 and our team were just inside the top half of Division 2. It was the time of Law, Charlton, Best, Stepney, Crerand et al. at United and we had nobody of any distinction. Ralph therefore said he would organise a bus if we could get the tickets. Many of us in our school year applied for tickets and we all got them except for one. It was going to be a good outing. Ralph stipulated that he did not want to see crates of booze on the bus, for although it was not an official school outing, he was still in charge.

The Saturday arrived and we all piled on to the bus armed with very heavy bags and rucksacks. Not a crate of beer in sight! We had hardly gone ten miles, when the first bottle was opened and some sandwiches were passed round too. It was approaching midday after all! This continued all the way to Manchester and by the time the bus was parked, there were some very unsteady youths. Final instructions were given and we were told that the bus would leave the bus stop in Piccadilly at 10pm, which would give us a chance to 'look round' and get something to eat.

Old Trafford was spectacular and there were a few thousand of our supporters in the ground. Scarves were being waved and the singing and football chants were deafening. It was a fantastic atmosphere. The joviality didn't last long, as United scored in the first ten minutes. However, our boys pressed hard and snatched an equaliser on the break just before half time. Very happy with the score so far, we tucked in to the customary pies and tea at half time. The second half started at a cracking pace, with both teams challenging. United had the pressure, but our boys were very quick on the counter attack and caused United some trouble at the back. From one of these counters, our boys scored and the away team end went berserk. United then piled forward and were left exposed at the back, which was just perfect as another counter attack brought another goal. Could it get any better? 1- 3 at Old Trafford was just sublime. If only we could hang on. With about five minutes to the end, we made our way to the exit, absolutely delirious and we caught a bus into the centre. We found a scruffy pub and piled in, virtually taking over the bar. The beer was flowing quite nicely and some of the locals were quite friendly, until one of them said, "Are you looking forward to the replay?"

"What replay? We won 3-1."

"No you didn't son. It was a 3-3 draw!"

"What? How was that possible? We left with five minutes to go. No-one could score two goals in the last five minutes!"

Apparently, during a United attack, one of the United players barged into our goalie and he clattered into a post. He was carried off the field with suspected concussion and as this was before substitutes, one of the midfielders had gone in goal and unfortunately, let in two goals in three minutes. We were devastated. The mood changed somewhat, but not for long as the landlord and his missus said they would do pie and peas for a small sum. That cheered us up a bit and so we proceeded to drown our sorrows.

Piccadilly was fairly busy and trying to cross roads after eleventeen pints proved very tricky. We finally found the bus park and before we clambered aboard, one of our group threw up at the back of the bus. Ralph heard the commotion and through his glazed eyes was heard to utter the immortal words,

"Have you been drinking?"

This caused even more hilarity and after the usual head count, we boarded the bus ready for the journey home.

Within five minutes there was not a sound. Everyone, including Ralph, was asleep. This lasted for about an hour or so and then the full bladders required emptying, so an unscheduled stop was made in a lay-by. It was a grand sight as about thirty youths spent a good few minutes relieving the pressure on their innards. It was not so good for Tom Robson, who accidently fell down the embankment that was currently being used as a urinal and got covered in pee. Fortunately, there was a double seat that was vacant, so he didn't have to share with anyone and he kept the smell to himself.

We arrived home in the very early hours and we all made our way home after a trip full of ups and downs.

Our team lost the replay.

Languages

One of our French teachers was a complete nutter and during the first French lesson of a new term, he entered the classroom with a new galvanised dustbin. He announced,

"From now on, we will speak only French. There will be no need for exercise books or text books, so as I come round, I would like you to put them in this dustbin. This will remain in the corner for the rest of the academic year, should you need them."

We were stunned as Joseph Fitzwilliam moved along the columns of desks and we put our French books in the dustbin. Jos also said,

"I will allow English to be spoken on the odd occasion that we need some vocabulary explaining. *Alors. Quel est votre nom? Vous répondez Je m'appelle Steve ou Pierre ou Alain etc.*"

So it went. Every lesson was French speaking. We actually learned a lot and we were getting quite good at speaking French, although the accent left a lot to be desired. However, when it came to the yearly exams, our results were not so good, in fact they were appalling. We could speak French quite well though. I was fortunate to get promotion to the A class and consequently when it came to a French lesson, I was hopeless at writing grammar. When asked why I was so bad, I explained in near perfect French what had happened during the last academic year with Jos Fitzwilliam. The others in the class were stunned too at my oral French.

This French speaking lark held me in good stead as one of the French Teachers organised a trip to Paris. This was supposed to be a cultural visit to the main tourist attractions. We all signed up for this as it required a flight as well, and many of our group had not been on an aeroplane. The trip was organised by the Head of French, William Blake (obviously not the poet and painter) and he was to be accompanied by three other members of staff, Jim Tweddle, Sheila Wilson and Doc. Halliday. Now we knew that Jim rather fancied Sheila, although there was no tenuous connection, they just seemed to get on a little too well! Doc Halliday was a jovial chap and was fond of a laugh and Blakey was a good sport too, although being in charge he had to lay the law down.

We flew in a twin engined turbo-prop of some description and it was all very exciting until we landed with a bump at Aéroport de Paris Nord (now Charles de Gaulle) and were whisked away by coach to our hotel in the centre. We were lucky enough to have the services of a tour guide, who was an eighteen year old female student called Nikki. She was blonde and beautiful and had all the class you would expect from a French lady. She was stunning. All the lads on the trip couldn't stop drooling! As we made our way to the hotel, she gave a commentary over the microphone about all the wonderful things in Paris, but we were not listening. We were quietly whispering to each other what manner of things we would like to get up to with Nikki on our arm or more importantly in our bed. We certainly were a randy lot!

The hotel was tall and narrow and had about five storeys with a small number of rooms on each floor. The rooms themselves were quite small, but that didn't matter as we were all excited because we were very close to the flesh pots of Paris. Before we headed off for dinner at the Cyrano restaurant, which was almost next door to the Moulin Rouge, we were given a severe talking to. There was to be no booze, either in rooms or outside. We would be given free time and we were not to abuse this. Red rags and bulls spring to mind!

The food in the restaurant was fantastic, but the meal seemed to go on for hours and hours. We were itching to sample the alcoholic cuisine and visit some of the more seedier establishments. At about 10pm the meal had finished and we all marched back to the hotel for a good nights' kip before the early start the following morning. We were all checked into our rooms and a final 'bon nuit' from Blakey should have heralded a few Zzzzz. However, we had other plans and within half an hour, there was a delicate tap on the door and some of the crew were collecting the rest of the drunks to sample the evening delights in Gay Paris.

We tiptoed down the stairs, bypassed the reception desk and disappeared into the Parisian air. We found a small bar just round the corner and the patron seemed friendly enough as we were spending our Francs on booze. Naturally, the crew shoved me to the front to converse with the patron and order the drinks as I was the best at speaking French. After a couple of drinks, we decided to make our way back as we did not want to outstay our welcome and get totally bladdered. As we sneaked in, the receptionist uttered the phrase without looking up,

"*Bonjour, messieurs du soir. Comment aimez-vous Paris la nuit?*"

"*Très bon merci. Bonne nuit.*"

On the last afternoon, we were given free time to buy souvenirs and presents etc on the condition that we were to have a group minimum of four, and it must include at least two girls. Blakey didn't want the girls wandering round on their own (with their miniskirts and full blouses) in this city of sin, especially not in the Pigalle district. This was no hardship as we were quite happy to accompany a number of buxom wenches. We arranged to meet in the foyer of the hotel at 2.30pm as the ladies were going up to their rooms to 'put on their faces and powder their nose'. Some of the boys went to the local bar for a swift one and I popped upstairs to change my shoes. As I was just putting on my shoes, there was a gentle knock on the door, it was Nikki.

"Allo. I have a small problem in my room, would you be so kind to help me out."

"*Bien sûr, Mademoiselle.*"

Off we went to her room, where she said that the zip on her dress was jammed and she could not undo it. I gulped and set to work on the zip, carefully moving her blonde locks out of the way. Her perfume was intoxicating and my hands started shaking a little. It *was* actually stuck and I had to use a bit of brute force to free the darned thing. As the zip was lowered, her dress fell to the floor and she turned around, revealing matching panties and a very full bra. I was stunned and just kept staring, probably with my mouth open while she moved towards me. I could definitely feel some stirrings in my nether region and it wasn't my pet hamster moving in my trouser pocket. Without taking her eyes from mine, she expertly removed my shirt and undid my trousers. With the minimum of fuss, we were kissing passionately on the bed and before long, she was on top, doing all the things we had imagined when we first set eyes on her.

Soon it was all over. Fortunately, it had lasted more than the customary five minutes that is usually associated with the male climax. Off she jumped and disappeared into the bathroom to refresh the parts beers cannot reach. I quickly got dressed and waited for her to appear. She simply said she had to report to her office, gave me a peck on the cheek and opened the door for me. As I walked down the corridor and stairs, I couldn't believe what had just happened! I popped into my room to have a wash and brush up, changed my shirt and rushed down to meet the others in the foyer, as I was a few minutes late. Naturally I was dying to tell the lads what had happened, but there were females present, so I decided to wait until later.

We had a great afternoon, using the metro and looking round by ourselves. We were in a group of about eight and it was all very jolly, even when the girls wanted to go into a lingerie shop. Naturally, I was pushed to the fore when there was negotiating to be done or asking questions/directions etc. We arrived back at the hotel in good time, so we dropped the girls off and then disappeared into our local bar. After we got the drinks in, I muttered to the other three,

"Lads. I've got something to tell you."

Davey, my room mate said, "Let me guess. You had rumpy pumpy with Nikki."

"How did you know?"

"We nearly all have! Was it the zip stuck on the dress routine, or was it I can't open the bathroom door routine?"

At this point we all convulsed in laughter. What were the odds of meeting up with a nymphomaniac tour guide?

Paris was magnificent and we did all the tourist bits, Notre Dame, Sacré Coeur, Arc de Triomphe, Les Invalides, various gardens and of course the Eiffel Tower. We managed to sneak out most nights and one night we gained entry into a sort of strip club, which we thought was a great laugh. None of the teachers could understand why we were so tired on a morning, but they hadn't been out 'til late most nights. For most of the time, I was the main interpreter and in a way I was pleased that the year with Jos Fitzwilliam was paying dividends. I could speak French better than any student on the trip and this really impressed the teachers at times.

I still did really poorly in my GCE French exam though.

Every school should have one!

Over the years it has been the custom in schools and unwritten law, to have a place set aside for the smoking fraternity. However, lately, with the increased awareness of cigarette related diseases and the various associated health issues, these have now been stopped. In the olden days in schools, it was very common to see the smokers gathered together, usually at the back of the sports hall, out of view of the rest of the school. Any teacher ventured there at his/her own risk and usually were dissuaded by their colleagues if they were new to the school.

We were fortunate at our school because the smokers had an amazing smoking sanctum in Ned's Shed. Ned was the groundsman and had been there for about six generations, fathers, grandfathers and even great grandfathers who attended the school knew about Ned's Shed. The age of Ned was a frequent discussion point, especially in the summer when he was sometimes spotted driving around on his motorised grass cutter. At other times, he was rarely seen. The first years (Year 7) were often told horror stories about groups of pupils who entered Ned's shed and were never seen again. Consequently, Ned's shed was the preserve of the older pupils (not the sixth form, as they were engaged in other activities).

If you were lucky enough to be invited (yes, invited) into Ned's shed at the furthest point away from school across the field, you went from a bright sunny day into a mysterious, dark cavern. The smell of creosote and paraffin was overpowering and as your eyes began to focus, you were greeted with the loudest and gruffest voice,

"Who are you? Did your dad come 'ere?"

If you managed to spit out an answer in your fright, you were then asked,

"Have you brought Ned a ciggy?"

If you answered negatively, there was a sinister growl and a riposte,

"You'd better remember two next time."

As your eyes became accustomed to the gloom, you would see various gardening implements, still in pristine condition as Ned had never used them. Also there would probably be half a dozen older boys sitting on oil drums etc. all smoking Woodbines or 'roll ups'. Ned had the only comfy chair, complete with a cushion, and he sat with his fag holding court. His paraffin stove kept the shed beautifully warm and he frequently warmed his rough 'workies' hands in between drags on his fag.

Now Ned was an authority on every subject you could think of. He had travelled the world. Apparently, (so he said) he could ask for sex in twelve languages and had made love thousands of times to the most beautiful and rich women. He had helped to write the Kama Sutra! What was that we all asked eagerly? When he explained, we were all very impressed! He could drink anyone under the table and he was a natural athlete in his youth and even coached Roger Bannister before he broke the four minute mile. His football career was cut short owing to the outbreak of the war. The war was not specified. We all thought it might have been the First World War, or even the Boer War. However, when he told us he had advised Winston Churchill on the Normandy landings, we knew it must have been World War Two.

On a cold winter morning at school, there was nothing more pleasurable than listening to one of Ned's stories in the warmth of his shed. If he was feeling particularly generous, he would make a brew and we would pass round the pint mug to have a sip. As a sanctuary for the smokers it worked a treat. No member of staff would deign to cross the field, let alone enter the inner sanctum. Of course we knew that all his stories were complete bollocks, but we thought of it as a community service, keeping an old geezer entertained and giving him company and a feeling of being wanted. Yes, we did our bit for humanity. One year, just before the Easter holidays, there was an almighty storm, which lasted about six hours during the night and early hours of the morning. There was thunder and lightning which lit up the night sky, but much worse were the severe gales which followed. It was frightening at times to hear tiles falling off the roof and smashing on the ground and also the sound of breaking glass. So it was, with tiredness in our eyes and a feeling of trepidation, we made our way to school the following morning. It was a bit of a disaster zone! Not only were there slates and tiles from the roof, but quite a number of broken panes of glass, mainly in one particular area. Now this was long before the "elf and safety" legislation and the do-gooders, so we were set to work clearing the debris in some classrooms, before lessons could commence. Obviously, one or two windows had to be boarded up, but generally after the break, everything continued as normal.

As usual at break, the smokers made their way across the field to Ned's shed. There it was, gone! Nothing was left apart from a rectangle of etiolated grass where the 'Temple' once stood. There was a stunned silence from the small gathering and after a while, they made their way in the opposite direction to end up behind the sports hall. No-one knew what happened to the 'Temple'. Worse still, no-one knew what had happened to Ned! He was never seen again. Maybe he actually lived in the shed and had been swallowed up by a tornado. We shall never know. Another sacred institution bit the dust.

Chapter 2

Mates days

Time misspent in youth is sometimes all the freedom one ever has – Anita Brookner

Choosing your friends is probably one of the most difficult, yet most influential things you can do as a teenager. I was greatly influenced by my friends as a youth, to the distraction of my studies. They seemed to have a good balance of work and play, but I seemed to lose this balance as I progressed through my teens. Jokingly, I often say I never grew up until I was thirty, that's when the children started arriving!

As a teenager, we did normal things like going to school, playing, falling in love, forming cliques, criticising adults, listening to music, itching to have sex, underage drinking etc. We often rebelled against some authority and once we had made a stand, we found it very difficult to back down, say sorry or accept we were wrong; this, I presume, is what teenagers are all about.

We were a very close knit group of friends. We all went to the same school and we met frequently outside of school for various 'events' as we lived within a mile or two of each other. We all used to give each other grief if we made a mistake relating a story or generally just chatting. There were frequent howls of laughter and red faces, but no-one seemed to be permanently offended or hold grudges. There was never a leader of the group, although some members of the clan seemed to dominate more than others, especially as their behaviour was more extreme.

During our early teens, we contented ourselves with playing footy and listening to music. Then a massive change took place. Voices changed, it became embarrassing to go into the communal showers at school, and we discovered the opposite sex. The latter was very strange as we had rarely looked at girls, and all of a sudden we changed from an all-boys grammar school to a co-ed school. There were girls in classrooms, separate changing rooms (obviously), lady teachers and boobies protruding from white blouses. All of a sudden the hormones kicked in and there was now competition to be the king pin and impress the girlies. It was very disconcerting and the change in attitude amongst the boys was incredible. We started to dress smartly, comb our hair, swagger a little down the corridors and most of all we had to learn how to address the girls. All of these things were alien to the younger boys, although we were often regaled with tales from the older boys and sixth formers about their sexual prowess.

Our first attempts at chatting up the girls were quite pathetic. However, we learned quickly and very soon we were trying to outdo each other in order to seek the attention of the opposite sex. The rate of development of girls and boys was very different; whereas the girls already had fully developed bits by the age of fourteen or fifteen, some of us boys were lagging behind. The growth of pubic hair seemed to be the criterion at which we were judged by our peers, as well as the size of todger. Some boys had sprouted before their teens and as well as deep voices, they were indeed in possession of finely thatched and well-structured todgers. They were first into the showers and regularly paraded their wares in front of lesser mortals.

None of this seemed to matter to our group of friends, as we remained the best of buddies despite all the hormonal distractions. Besides, the girls in our classes already seemed to be forming relationships with boys two years above us, so we just had to bide our time.

In our mid-teens, we thought it was very manly to consume alcohol, mainly in the form of beer. Wine had not been invented yet! At every opportunity from fifteen onwards, we tried to sneak in a few bottles of the local ales and consume them at one or others houses, whilst listening to music. It was quite nice getting 'squiffy', although we could not afford to get completely smashed. The excitement was for one person (who looked the oldest) to pop into the local off licence and purchase a couple of bottles for each of us. This was also good training for telling lies, as we were always asked if we were old enough and we always said that we were. This habit seemed to continue for ages, and we gladly spent our pocket money or newspaper round money on bottles of beer to drink in a friend's house, while comparing the 'attributes' of the girls at school.

On reaching sixteen and beyond, it was time to take the big plunge and try and get served in a pub. This had been discussed for ages and we finally made plans to give it a go. For this momentous event, we all dressed up in our best gear and really looked smart – Ooo we did scrub up well. We decided to head for the older part of town where there were a lot of old local pubs, perhaps some of them not doing so well. We chose one called the Wagon and Horses Hotel one Friday night and in we went. We had decided not to go into the bar, as we were sure the local blokes would have given us grief. Instead we chose the lounge, which was waitress service, the waitress being about ninety-two. We sat down around a table and pressed the bell for service. It was a good job some of us were wearing brown trousers! In staggered Betty the waitress with a tray in one hand swinging by her side.

"Evening lads. What can I get you?"

"Six pints of 'best' please."

"Are you all eighteen?"

"Ah yes!" came the reply from the six of us.

"Righto. I'll not be a minute" and off she toddled.

That was the difficult bit. After a few minutes, Betty came back with the tray of drinks. All proper straight glasses, just like we'd seen on Coronation Street.

We gave her some money and asked her, "Will yer be having one yourself?"

"Eee that's very kind lads. I'll have half a stout if that's alright?"

"Yes, that's fine!"

We couldn't believe our luck. We had been served and were supping real draught beer from a proper glass. We chatted and laughed excitedly, before ordering another one. Before the next round arrived, about six elderly ladies came in and sat opposite us. After the usual hellos etc. we got talking to them and it seemed they went in there every Friday night after the bingo. They were nice enough and seemed to be enjoying their refreshment. After finishing our second pint, we said our goodbyes to Betty and the bingo girls and headed off to the bus station in the rain. It didn't matter that it was raining and we got wet, we had just been served in a pub! We were euphoric. After piling on the bus, we decided to try again next week and see if we could get away with it two weeks in a row.

At school that week, we could talk of nothing else. The lessons seemed to drag on forever and homework was the least of our worries, as we looked forward to the Friday night down the pub. Just saying it made us sound all grown up and finally Friday came around. As before, we all met at the bus stop and we got off at the town centre. After a short walk, we entered the lounge of the Wagon and Horses and were greeted by Betty. Drinks ordered, we relaxed and started talking about our favourite subject, girls. As usual about 9pm, the bingo crew came in and it was like meeting long lost relatives' – not quite hugs and kisses, but they did seem pleased to see us. As we talked, one of the lads let slip that we were still at school, which led to frowns from the ladies. When we explained that we were doing A levels, the atmosphere relaxed again. It seemed as though we had been coming here for years. After the sixth or seventh time, one of the lads was showing the ladies some photographs of the harbour in days gone by, when in walked a police constable!

"Evening all. Everybody alright? Just having a look round a few pubs, as there have been reports of disorderly youths, obviously not here though!" And with that he was gone.

"Are you sure you lads are all of age?"

"Oh yes" came the reply. We were doubly chuffed. We had just passed the Constabulary test.

Friday nights at the Wagon and Horses became a tradition and we had guest visits from some of our schoolmates. One evening was exciting, as one of the blokes in the bar stuck his head round the door and asked if any of us were good at darts, as there was a darts match and one member of the team hadn't turned up. Crazily, one of our crew, Rob, used to play darts all the time at home as he had his own dartboard. He was volunteered by the rest of us and we went through into the bar to watch. It seems we were 'regulars' now! We were even more accepted as Rob played a blinder and beat the opposition number one on the last game to win the match. The blokes in the bar were well chuffed and bought us beers all round.

As we staggered out of the pub to the bus station, about an hour later than usual and with twice the volume of beer inside of us, we hoped that this scenario would go on forever. Needless to say it didn't. One of our excursions to the off-licence on a Saturday evening resulted in the purchase of a crate of local beer. This was then carried to Brads' house, where it would be consumed with great vigour whilst listening to records of our time. A pleasant evening was forthcoming and there were lots of relevant discussions, mainly about females. It was decided, after a large quantity of ale, that we would have to do something about the 'lack of female' situation and therefore we would have to get off our arses and get stuck in. Fortunately, Mr Bradley came in with some of his potent home brew and gave us some good advice.

"Always have a couple of pints of home brew before attempting to chat up the ladies. It will help you lose your inhibitions and give you confidence."

Thank you Mr Bradley! What he forgot to mention was that his homebrew was at least twice as strong as the local ale we were used to, and consequently there were some disastrous consequences.

Following the good advice, one particular Friday we consumed a couple of pints of home brew and then made our way into town to the Locarno Ballroom or the Mecca as we used to call it. We had a couple of beers on the way too and together with the ultra-brew, it was just starting to kick in big time. We thought we were invincible and that we would have girls falling at our feet. Instead, we were falling at their feet. The home brew was having a mega effect and we were falling about all over. Amazingly as the night wore on and the alcohol wore off, we all managed to pull. However, the best girls were gone and this gave rise to a future event, The Horrors Competition.

The rules were simple. One of the gang was elected chairman and he went around observing the young ladies we were dancing with and issuing points for various attributes. At the end of the evening, the chap with the most points got free beer at the next outing supplied by the rest. Points were awarded as follows:-

2 points long greasy hair
1 point pigeon toes
2 points National Health specs
3 points cast in the eye
5 points cross eyes
2 points fat
3 points very fat
2 points skinny

2 points no boobs
5 points smooch
8 points snog
2 points can't dance
Etc.

Now this might have seemed cruel to the unaccustomed eye, but these girls went along to this cattle market in the hope of meeting Mr Right. It was never going to happen! Imagine their delight when five handsome lads in their prime asked them to dance and cuddled up close for the slow numbers. We were just doing a social service, which some of them might remember for a week or two and hopefully may give them a warm glow.

We were all quite good at sport and despite our alcoholic excesses, we all played for various school and local teams in a number of different sports. Amazingly, we all came together to form a ten pin bowling league at the local bowling alley. There were about twelve teams in all and although we were not all top bowlers, we could hold our own against most teams. Towards the end of the season, there were various trophies to play for and our team of 'Reprobates' (yes that was our name), were lying second and in with a chance of the title and a trophy each. The last session would decide all, as we were playing a mid-table team and the leaders were playing the current third place team. We had to win by a decent margin to win the title.

Before we played the final match, we were invited to Brad's' house to have a glass of homebrew 'to settle the nerves'. When we arrived, Brad had already started settling his nerves and we eagerly followed suit. After a couple of pints, our nerves had definitely been settled and we were then required to lose our inhibitions with another beer or two. By the time we boarded the bus to the bowling alley, we had definitely lost all our inhibitions and various other things.

After changing our shoes at the bowling centre, we found our lane and our opponents and got straight on with the match. Our arch rivals were two lanes away, so we could keep a check on the scores. It all started magnificently, with two of our team getting three strikes in a row. We were all bowling superbly and were dead certs to win the league. As we got towards the end of the frame, people were starting to gather behind us to watch the final few frames. There was no pressure here, as we had supped enough homebrew to quell anything that was remotely nervy. Then disaster! Was it the extra homebrew that Brad had before we arrived or was it just a terrible blip? Whatever it was, Brad walked up to bowl his eighth frame and the ball seemed to stick in his fingers as he delivered it. Not only did it go up in the air, but it also veered hard left and bumped over into the next lane, where it demolished nine out of the ten pins. Howls of laughter followed this event and it took a good five minutes for the ruckus to subside. By this time, our confidence was shot and Brad's' second ball only scored three. Incredibly, all our confidence was shattered and we bowled abysmally to the end of the frame. We scraped the match, but only just. However, our competitors had seen this debacle and this gave them confidence to not only thrash their opponents, but to lift the trophy and the title. What a bummer after the festivities died down and our cries of 'bastards' were drowned out by the applause. We got together and decided to walk into the town centre and drown our sorrows. It didn't take much to get us well and truly poleaxed, as we already had a good level of blood in our alcohol. After the final drink, we made our way to the bus and climbed on the double decker. There were not many people on the bus, which was just as well as one of our crew moved to the back seat and urinated as he was bursting and couldn't hold back. The conductor heard the row and came upstairs to see what was going on. When he saw what had happened, he stopped the bus and kicked us all off. I didn't blame him; we were way out of order! It was a good job we only had about a mile to walk home.

Well, what a way to end a disastrous evening. As the teenage years progressed, we all had different girlfriends and we often met up to make a foursome or a sixsome. We were always passionately in love with our current girlfriends and we often had discussions about 'how far we got!' We always exaggerated about what had happened, but it was good for the ego and we all knew each of us was exaggerating. No matter how complicated things became, we all remained very close friends and there was one time when girlfriends were not invited – the Sunday lunchtime sessions at the Working Men's Club.

It was the custom that men only went to the 'club' on a Sunday lunchtime and upstairs in the concert room there was a real treat – strippers.

Yes. As the concert chairman asked us to fill our glasses, we waited for the debacle to start. Each stripper was accompanied by the resident duo, Tom on the organ (electric) and Jacky on the drums as the announcement was made, "Gentlemen! Please give the best of order for Miss Manchester 1963."

This announcement was followed by rapturous applause as all the old blokes gave their full attention. Finally, the music started, Tom and Jacky were in full flow and Miss Manchester '63 appeared in a very revealing outfit. I don't think it was Miss Manchester 1963, more like Miss Manchester '43. All the wrinkles and varicose veins etc. were blotted out by make-up and crafty lighting. The old blokes were really revving, whereas us youngsters were having a real good laugh and were frequently 'shushed' by the older crew. On many occasions, Jacky could be seen getting more and more inebriated as his glasses would slowly fall down his nose as he was staring so hard. On one occasion, he was stretching so hard to see the strippers' bits that he fell of his stool into his drum kit.

The best stripper was on last and usually she was quite reasonable. By the time she came on, however, we had had too much beer and we didn't give a damn. The beer itself was very cheap, almost half the price of normal ale, but it wasn't strong and it made you go to the loo frequently.

There was nothing like a few pints and a stripper or two to set you up for your Sunday dinner at about 2.30pm.

Occasionally at the club there was a decent group on and this attracted youths from far and wide. On one particular occasion, there were two rival factions at opposite ends of the concert hall, and they were separated by two rows of tables and chairs which the 'normal' people occupied. So we were in the middle of this potential holocaust and throughout the evening as the band played, they continued to look daggers at each other. It was noticeable too, that neither group went to the toilet on their own. Three or four would always go together in case of fisticuffs from their rivals, who might have been in the toilet at the same time. The management seemed totally unaware of this and there was an uneasy truce throughout the evening. Towards the end as 'last orders' was called, someone shouted something across the room, as the beer had started to take effect and there was more bravado from the assembled groups. All of a sudden it kicked off and before you could say, "Giz another drink!" bottles and glasses were being exchanged in flight across the room. The group continued playing and the concert chairman and committee ran for cover, no doubt phoning the police from the office.

The mayhem continued. We were still in the middle of all of this and glasses and bottles were whizzing above our heads, we kept ourselves low near the table. All of a sudden someone yelled, "Look out!"

As I turned, a brown ale bottle hit me slap bang in the mouth. I don't remember much after that apart from being herded into a van with a load of other youths. I really came round at the local nick after my blood stained face was attended to by a medic of some kind. The next thing I remember is waking up in a cell next to an unknown youth and my face was the size of Saturn. This was not good as I couldn't speak. A burly policeman came and unlocked the cell and herded us and others out along a corridor and up some stairs into a courtroom! What was going on?

Apparently, we were all being charged with being drunk and disorderly and causing some kind of affray.

Each youth was asked his name and how did he plead. Everyone said they were guilty and when it was my turn, as I couldn't speak, the bloke in the chair asked the others who I was and was I guilty? They all said they hadn't a clue who I was, so I was taken away to a doctor's surgery and patched up properly. Needless to say, I had lost my two front teeth and my face was a real mess for days. It sort of took the shine off going to the club, but I still have the false teeth.

On rare occasions when we all didn't have girlfriends, it came as no surprise that the lads would have a Saturday night out in town together. This mainly consisted of moving from pub to pub in the hope of finding new love. 'Chat up lines' were few and far between and we all tried to impress the ladies with our sparkling wit and repartee. This was not always successful. However, we often had the pleasure of escorting the ladies to the bus station, where a quick grope and saliva swapping ensued. This activity nearly always occurred when the effect of large quantities of alcohol rendered the ladies a bit squiffy.

One evening proved very unsuccessful with the ladies and so we were wending our way back to the bus station for the bus home. We were a bit miserable as only one of our group was escorting a young lady to the bus station, and her friend did not want to know any of us, so she walked on her own about ten paces behind the couple. The rest of us followed a good way behind. Suddenly, one of the gang said he was desperate to go for a pee. This was very inconvenient as we were in the middle of a shopping precinct and there were no toilets around. He told us to go on ahead and he would catch up as he was going to relieve himself in an alcove next to a shop. After a few minutes, he came charging up the street trying to zip up his fly and was being chased by girls and youths. He ran past us and we acted surprised as we casually blocked the pavement which prevented the pursuing group from following. When we asked what the matter was, they said they were having a coke and a burger in a Wimpy bar when that youth came to the side window, got out his todger and started to pee against the smoked glass window. That's why they were chasing him. It was a good job we had blocked the pavement and he duly escaped their wrath, as he must have caught the early bus.

When we questioned him later, he said he had not seen the lights inside the Wimpy Bar, as the glass was very dark. He should have gone for a pee before he left the pub!

Teenagers are notorious for being stubborn. Even if proven wrong on a particular subject, they are more prone to stomp off in a huff than back down and say sorry. Our group of lads were no exception. It happened many times, but no-one bore any grudges and it was readily forgotten apart from one time on a Christmas Eve. We were all having a drink in our local pub on Christmas Eve and for once we were all legal. The beer was flowing and everyone was in a very happy frame of mind. There were the usual faux pas and that evening there was no huffiness, just plenty of laughter and hilarity. We had got to the pub early and claimed our favourite seat in the corner. Florrie was on hand to keep us topped up. She belied her sixty-three years and romped about the very large lounge like a fifty-five year old. The lounge was quite full and standing at the bar was an off duty policeman, sadly called PC Pigg. One or two of our company had had dealings with this officer before, and he was not known for his speed of thought or verbosity. Perhaps he should have been called PC Plod as this would have been very appropriate.

On one occasion he was made to look an idiot by attempting to arrest the wrong person in the pub. Everyone laughed in the pub and he had to slink out, humiliated. Tonight he was having a drink with a colleague, who was also a member of the blue brigade. This was like red rag to a bull to a couple of our crew – two coppers in one room, an opportunity for fun and games! The noise and laughter at our table got louder and louder as the beer went down, and it was noticeable that PC Pigg was constantly looking our way. His colleague seemed totally disinterested in the noise in the corner. As the night progressed, we got louder and louder and the jokes (mainly about policemen) were coming thick and fast.

Police: "Do you know why I pulled you over?" Me: "Because you were bored and wanted someone to talk to?"

At this point the corner erupted and one of the gang had his mouth round the glass, just about ready to take a mouthful when the punch line was delivered. He accidently bit down on the glass and part of the edge broke off. We all laughed loudly.

At this point, PC Pigg strode over, bent down and looked my friend in the eye.

"I saw you chew that glass on purpose."

There was a momentary silence and the whole of the pub, including Florrie and the bar staff, erupted in laughter. PC Pigg had done it again! There was even more laughter when he asked the landlady if she wished to press charges for wilful damage. We were rolling about on our seats and even the old folk were having the time of their lives. It certainly was a Merry Christmas. When the laughter finally subsided, we noticed that PC Pigg had left the premises.

"I bet he's waiting for me outside," said my friend. "Well I'll give him something to wait for," he said. We never thought any more about this and all too soon closing time loomed. We all went to the toilet except the one friend who had 'chewed the glass.' When we came out of the toilet, he was nowhere to be found. We looked inside and outside, up the road and down the road, in fact everywhere we could think of. As we stood outside the pub, one of our mates said, "I hope he's not going to do anything stupid!"

At that point, a Jaguar roared out of the car park driven by our missing friend. What was going on? He didn't have a Jag! Surely he hadn't nicked it? Was he going mad? He had drunk at least eight pints of ale! What on earth could we do?

The Jag quickly disappeared out of sight and we thought we had better go round and tell our friends' parents what was going on. We did this and naturally his father was delighted to hear that his son had drunk eight pints of ale, then stolen a car and sped off.

The story unfolded a few days later

Apparently, as the Jag sped off, it was in a thirty mile an hour limit and it had accelerated up to about fifty. It was soon spotted by a police car, who gave chase. The Jag headed off along a straight minor road towards the countryside and must have clocked a ton.

The police car had called for assistance and a road block was arranged a few miles up ahead. After a couple of minutes, the Jag reached the road block and tried to squeeze past, but there was no gap to do this and so it was pulled up. Our friend was arrested and carted off to the local nick where his father was already waiting for him. He was cautioned and put in the cells as some paperwork was being filled out. His father was allowed to see him and asked him why he had done it.

"Not saying anything to anybody!"

"But why did you do it after drinking so much as well?

"Not saying anything to anybody!"

At that point, a policeman entered and asked him to sign something.

"I'm not signing anything!"

"If you sign this," said the officer, "you will be free to go for the time being. It's Christmas and you should be at home with your family."

"I'm not signing anything!"

"C'mon young man. Your dad has given us all your particulars. Just sign here and he will take you home."

"I'm not signing anything!"

"You're only hurting yourself and your family. It's now after midnight and it's officially Christmas Day."

"I'm not signing anything!"

His father tried to get him to sign the release but to no avail.

"I'm not signing anything!"

At about 2 am on Christmas morning after many efforts of persuasion, the policeman finally lost patience and yelled,

"Get him out of here!"

His father took him home and no charges were pressed. The police were just so glad to get him out of the station.

Merry Christmas!

Chapter 3

College Days

> It is a thousand times better to have common sense without education than to have education without common sense.
> Robert green Ingersoll

In the good old days, it was assumed that when one completed their time at school, one would then move on to higher education in the form of University, College, Polytechnic or Technical College. Each had its merits and each was dependent on the academic standard of its students. Nowadays, they are all lumped together and called 'Uni', giving out a degree for the correct spelling of one's name on a single exam paper coupled with course work, which is usually stolen via the interweb. Failure is rarely an option, as it rarely happens. Consequently, most people over the age of twenty-one have some nice pieces of paper with a degree on it. Are we therefore developing a super elite and super intelligent society? It would be nice to think so, but a bit naive.

Like most teenagers, I had little idea what to do after schooling had finished. As mentioned earlier, I had brochures and papers thrust in front of me to help me decide on the course of my further study. Did I want to become a doctor, nuclear physicist, airline pilot, bricklayer, television producer etc.? Well, my grades were not brilliant, so it ruled out many of the options and I had to decide on another way to choose my further education. As a 'late developer', I had discovered fairly recently the pleasures of females and alcohol. This led to a massive downward spiral in my studies, but increased my popularity with the opposite sex massively. I therefore decided to base my further education on the number of females at the aforesaid establishment, and also sync this with the number of bars on campus and the nearby vicinity. This, I hoped, would lead to some kind of further qualification to enable me to make a decent living. At the same time, it would give me the opportunity to have a lot of fun and to practise my new found skills in debauchery.

As the selection process got underway, I decided to rule out small towns and rural establishments and opted for the larger cities, Sheffield, London, Birmingham, Manchester and Liverpool etc. These prospectuses were scoured at every available opportunity and amazingly, I found a college in Liverpool that had places for six hundred females (approx.) and two hundred males. This looked very good indeed, even when the 'knitting circle' and the 'blokes at home' groups were removed from the equation. Consequently, the application form was filled out and sent. Within a week, a reply was obtained and I had an interview for the new academic year, which started in just over a month. Hardly time to pack my condoms! Surprisingly too, after the interview, where I said all the right things, I was offered a place. Preparations began in earnest. New gear was bought from all the trendy shops in town and I had already been growing my hair and a bit of fuzz was developing on my upper lip, just the ticket for the late sixties/very early seventies. Oh, I also bought a writing pad and a new pen and pencil. Now that I was going to become a proper student, I had to show willing! I had a reasonable amount of cash as I had been working all summer in between leching and drinking, and was ready to take the plunge into higher education.

I was placed in digs in a posh end of Liverpool (yes, there was such a place), just down the road from where John Lennon was brought up, and the infamous Strawberry Fields was not far away either. My roommate was a Lancashire lad who had Russian parentage. Funnily enough, he had the same vision as I did when applying for a place, but his girlfriend already had a place there and so he was rarely seen at beddy byes time. I just about had the run of the place. It was quite a nice house and the landlord and lady were brilliant. They lived there as well and were very caring and supportive. They always played loud music in their bedroom when having sex, as they knew I would be hard at work on my assignments (not). One of them must have been a screamer, hence the loud music. All in all, it was a good place to be and I had a good feeling about digs, college, lectures and the social life.

All meals (apart from breakfast) were taken in college and the dining hall was very grand, with heavy oak tables and chairs. At coffee on the first morning, all the third year male students sat near the back by the entrance. This was a fantastic vantage point for eyeing up the new talent in the first year, and just occasionally massive applause rang out as a really good looking girl entered. This was very embarrassing for the female concerned, but some took it in good spirit and flashed the V signs to the rabble at the back, whilst grinning excitedly. After lectures had finished for the day, quite a lot of folk congregated in the college bar, where a few of the third year tried another wheeze. As the first year males went to the bar, they were hijacked by the elder students and told it was customary for the 'newbies' to buy a drink for the old 'uns. Quite a few 'newbies' got clobbered for this, but when my roommate and I were approached with this offer, I replied in a very loud voice, "I would be delighted to buy you a drink, as I only ever buy drinks for ladies!"

This caused a lot of hilarity and I was immediately accepted by the crowd.

So began my first adventure into college life as the 'newbies' finally got into the routine of missing lectures and lying in bed until the afternoon, a number of incidents coloured the otherwise drab scene. After a few weeks, we began to set our own hidden agenda. Friday was 'Education Day' for us and we would spend all of the morning listening to some 'notable' speaker droning on about Piaget, Rousseau, Steiner et al and then in the afternoon, we spent time with our education tutors discussing the said philosophy. We decided to have a competition amongst some of the groups, whereby the group who kept the education lecturer off the subject for the longest, had a drink bought for them in the bar afterwards. Obviously, we were honest about the length of time and we even had an official timekeeper in every group. Lectures finished at 6pm, so everyone made their way to the bar to see who had won. It was a wonderful sight to see the various groups come through the door and say their time loudly. Any lecturers who had popped in for a swift one, had no idea what was going on as one by one, each group appeared and said a number (in minutes). For most of the term, it was a close run thing between our group and another group which had a lot of 'footy lads' in it, and their tutor was a keen Liverpool supporter.

We had two Welsh girls in our group, Blodwyn and Ceinwen who were so Welsh, they were almost incomprehensible when they spoke. Now Blodwyn apparently means in Welsh 'white flower', while Ceinwen comes from the Welsh words 'lovely and fair'. Blodwyn was certainly not a white flower and Ceinwen definitely wasn't lovely and fair. If they had auditioned for the parts of two of the three ugly sisters, they would have had no competition, even without make-up. They were both from Welsh speaking families and would start a sentence in English and drift into Welsh half way through. It was even worse when they had had a drink! However, these two girls were our secret weapon. Whenever we were running out of distracting talk in the education tutorials, they stepped in and totally confused everybody, including our tutor, with their chat. The final tutorial of the term was a classic, as our tutor was having a new kitchen fitted for the festive season. This gave us massive scope to keep off the subject of education and when Ceinwen related that her father was a joiner who fitted kitchens, she kept us enthralled for ages with her crazy accent and tales of 'mitres, tongue and grooves, single and double base units etc. Out of ten Friday tutorials in the first term, we were the victors on seven occasions.

Our College had lots of characters. Some were just OTT. Others were still notable, but went about their business quietly. One such chap was Davey. Davey was over six feet tall and nearly the same round the middle. Every day he wore a bright green woolly jumper with new sleeves from the elbow down, in a slightly different colour to the rest of his jumper. He was a pleasant lad, but had one or two tricks up his newly knitted sleeve! In the bar in the evening, someone would take out a packet of ciggies and hand them round, knowing that everyone would do the same. Well, not everyone! When it was Davey's turn to 'flash the ash', he would reach into his pocket and pull out a packet with only one in.

"Sorry lads, only one left."

This was the usual phrase heard at least once every Saturday night. What used to happen was, that Davey went to the toilet and put a single ciggy in a packet and stashed the rest in his coat pocket in the cloakroom. It took a while for us to catch on, as the alcohol was flowing and no-one paid much attention to it. Eventually, we cured him of this, as someone realised what was going on and also went to the toilet, where he grabbed the full packet from Davey's coat before returning triumphant to the bar, "Hey lads! Look what I found on the cloakroom floor!"

Of course, Davey couldn't say anything, because he 'hadn't got any ciggies!'

Another stunt he used to pull was when he was actually living in College. He used to pop down to the bar as usual, order a beer and then while he was stood waiting for his change, he would frisk his pockets and utter,

"Oh damn. I've left my ciggies up in my room. You couldn't let me have one now and I'll pop up in a bit to retrieve them."

Well this was fine for the first twenty or thirty times and then we cottoned on and told him politely to bugger off.

It was amazing, that when he scraped through his final exams, doing Political Studies, he got a job as Head of Music in a really rough school, as no-one wanted the job. He was amply qualified to teach music, as he tinkered a bit on a guitar and he could sing quite well. That same year, he came up on the football pools and won a fortune. He was then nicknamed 'the lucky rich fat pig.'

The following year, we all had a college reunion in the college bar and loads of people turned up. As we looked out of the window, this Bentley (or similar) turned up and out got the lucky rich fat pig, wearing the same green jumper he had always worn. As he made his way to the bar and ordered his drink, he frisked his pockets and said,

"Can anyone lend me a fag, I must have left mine in the car!"

The crowd collapsed in a heap laughing.

During the summer term, the football season had finished and we had to amuse ourselves in other ways, whilst supposedly revising for the imminent end of year exams. One bright spark came up with the unusual game of 'fanny football'. This game was actually more like golf than football, as there was a definite 'course' to follow. However, there were no golf balls, just a football each and an obstacle course to get the ball in a 'hole'.

1st hole par 4: From the goal post on the playing field, kick the ball over the four metre hedge into the rose garden. (Dropped ball and lose one stroke if it landed in the rose bushes). From the grass path between the roses, kick the ball diagonally over a second four metre hedge and then kick it back along the opposite diagonal over yet another hedge into a quadrangle. At the far corner of the quadrangle was a small pond which was 'the hole'. Kicking the ball over the zig zag of hedges was to avoid the accommodation block, which was three storeys high.

2nd hole par 3: From the pond, kick the ball high and hard to clear two hedges and two paths. (Dropped ball and lose one stroke if the ball entered the science block). From the main driveway, chip the ball onto the small lawn. The bird bath in the centre of the lawn is the hole.

The other seven holes followed much the same pattern, over hedges and gates, along paths, etc. The longest hole was a classic par 5. The main college building was in the shape of an H and the object was to hoof the ball along the corridors to the very end, across the inside quadrangle, past the Principal's office and out the opposite end, finally wedging the ball between the bicycles in the bike sheds. These nine holes took us all through the college and grounds, only missing out on the 'sick bay' (medical centre), admin offices and the staff common room. There was some discussion whether the bell tower would play a part in this, but it was decided not to include this as it would be pushing it too far.

Foursomes was the most popular format, although some of the best scores appeared during two player games. Most players were very happy with a score in the low thirties. Enter the lucky, rich, fat, pig hole 1: Usual kick over the four metre hedge into the rose garden. Not only did it land directly on the grass, but was in a perfect position for shots 2 and 3, the diagonals. But with his usual aplomb and huge bulk, he decided to have a go at clearing the accommodation block, which no-one had done before. He took a run and hoofed the ball as high and as hard as he could. You could hear the laughter for miles, as the ball disappeared through an open window on the top floor of the block. The referee was called in to decide the penalty as we all trudged round to find the ball and retrieve it from someone's room. When we got to the front door, it was wide open. When we found the room with the open window, that door was wide open too and there was no sign of the ball! Could it be that the ball had flown through the window and gone out of the study door? If this had happened, it may have gone down the stairs and out of the front door. Surely not? The grounds were scoured and someone spotted the ball floating in the pond. It was an eagle; two under par, something that had never been done before. That hole by the lucky rich fat pig is still legendary in games of fanny football. Many have tried to equal this feat, but none have succeeded.

These college days were before the invention of computerised electronic games and consequently, we had to amuse ourselves with other games. The table footy was always monopolised by the footy crowd, the table tennis table was mostly monopolised by the table tennis team (who were bloody good and played in the premier division on Merseyside), the pool table, which was monopolised, strangely enough by the girlies and the pinball machine which was monopolised by me. I already had practised many times on a pin ball machine at home, as I used to jam a special coin in it to get free games. I loved it. A real pinball wizard! I used to rack up lots of free games and when I was tired of playing, I would donate the games to the crowd who had gathered to watch the expert. It was to become an obsession, as I sometimes forgot all sense of time and was often late for lectures and one time even missed lunch! I couldn't seem to get enough of it. When the rest of the gang were drinking coffee etc. in the union bar, I would 'just nip out for a quick game.'

As I mentioned, there were about six hundred females and two hundred males in college. Therefore the odds of a reasonable looking bloke (or even an ugly git for that matter) picking up a very smart looking girl were quite high. Like any healthy community, various liaisons blossomed. After all, the testosterone was present in vast quantities as there were a lot of PE blokes running around in skimpy shorts, baring their chests to anyone who would care to watch. Even some of the knitting circle would venture down to the bar for a shandy or two on a Saturday night, in the hope of being ravaged by these very fit males.

One evening I was in the college bar and noticed a couple of young ladies. One was a stunner and her mate wasn't bad either! I had already noted the stunner previously and was very impressed with her long dark hair, big brown eyes and her tall curvaceous figure. She seemed quite upset and as the bar was not particularly crowded, I wandered over to offer my assistance in any way I could, particularly if it involved walking her back to her study bedroom. However, she had just been informed, by letter, that a bloke from home had dumped her – very sad news. But after a few drinks, she seemed to be getting over it, especially as I had given the nod to one of my mates to keep her friend company. At the end of the evening, we did the noble thing and escorted the young ladies back to their rooms. I arranged to meet Linda that Saturday evening and have a couple of drinks.

After our footy match on Saturday, I got showered and smartened up ready for my date. I just popped over to the coffee bar and as there was no-one on the pin ball table, I decided to have a quick game. About three hours later, I suddenly realised I should have met Linda about half an hour ago. I left all my free games and legged it to the bar to find her deep in conversation with one of the footy lads. Apparently, she had wandered over to the coffee bar when I didn't show, but I was so intent on the pin ball table, I never knew she was there. As I looked at her, she just shrugged her shoulders and carried on the conversation. It won't be the first time I would get jilted, unless I gave up pin balling.

The college had a strong legacy of sport, even before the blokes arrived. We had one of the first female rugby teams in a competitive league and they had a bit of a reputation. When the blokes arrived in the mid-sixties, footy became the dominant sport for them and eventually three teams were formed to compete in the Liverpool league, of which there were twelve leagues. The college first team were mainly the PE guys with one or two others. The second and third teams were mainly the other blokes who liked a good kick around. If you were in the third team and in the eleventh division of the Liverpool League, that is mainly what you got.

The third team was full of characters and mainly useless players, who used to brag about their football prowess until they appeared on the field. Then things sometimes got a little scary. One chap in the third team was a gangly youth called Dicko. He was over six feet tall and couldn't have weighed more than ten stone. Apart from his short sight (he frequently had specs sellotaped to his head), he had two left feet and couldn't kick a ball straight if his life depended on it. He played centre forward. He hardly ran in any match and spent much of the time standing by the centre circle. At the end of each match, he could be seen running for the bath in his immaculate kit (there was only one bath, the rest of us had showers). It was the only time he could be seen running!

After one particular gruelling match, Dicko, as usual, legged it to get the only bath. We were all slightly brassed off, as we had given our all and were covered in mud and filth and could hardly walk, let alone run to the changers. Seeing Dicko legging it to get the only bath in his pristine kit, was not what we wanted to see. By the time we got to the changers, we could hear Dicko singing his heart out. He obviously had plenty of strength left! One of the guys then had a brilliant idea! We found some empty, solid waste bins and filled them with cold water before sneaking into the bath area. There was a wooden cubicle around the bath for privacy, so he never heard or saw us approaching. Three of us lined up and on the silent count of three, we threw the water over the cubicle and retreated very quickly. The language that came from within was incredible. The following home match had exactly the same consequences and the same verbal abuse. The match after that, Dicko was seen walking off the field and when asked if he was going to take the bath, he just indicated that he was giving the bath a miss and someone else could have it. How noble we thought. In one particular match however he shone like a beacon in the dark but the season was not very successful, three wins, six draws and six losses. Not disastrous, just not up to scratch. It was the penultimate match of the season and Dicko, even though he was centre forward, hadn't scored one. Not that there was much scoring anyway, with four 0-0 draws and two 1-0 wins to our credit. This particular match was against the bottom club, who were also renowned for their bone crunching tackles and their expert fouls. The game got off to a bad start as our goalie let one through his legs after about ten minutes, and the score stayed like that until half time. Then the miracle happened. Dicko got a hat trick.

Goal 1: We had a corner and I took it. As I swung the ball over into the penalty area, I saw Dicko rise above everyone else and completely miss the ball. As he swung his head in thin air, his glasses fell off. He bent down to retrieve them, when another of our team wellied the ball goalwards. As luck would have it, it bounced off Dicko's bum and ricocheted into the goal. Brilliant.

Goal 2: I'm speeding down the right and spot Dicko actually running into the penalty area. Just as I cross the ball, Dicko is tripped up by one of the opposition. As the expletives pour from his mouth, he falls forward, he meets the ball with his forehead and pings it into the goal. The best diving header I've ever seen.

Goal 3: Confidence is sky high, time for some intricate dribbling in the penalty area from Dicko. Melee of players around Dicko, who has the ball tucked somewhere by his boot, trying his hardest to burst through the line of gorillas. The centre half grabs Dicko's shirt or shorts and they both rip, with his shorts coming off in his hand. Everyone rolls about laughing, except Dicko, who powers and stumbles his way over the line with the football and his penis and testicles swinging freely. The centre half was still holding Dicko's shorts and half a shirt. Game restarted after five minutes, once everyone had stopped laughing.

Final score 3-1. You couldn't make it up.

As the footy season progressed, there was some argument over the fitness of some players and also some of the more 'talented' players just expected to turn up on Saturday afternoon and play in the first team. There was a lot of disgruntlement, as some of these guys although they were undoubtedly talented, did not run for the full ninety minutes, whereas many who did not quite make the firsts, would run until they bust a gut. Meetings were held and it was decided, by general consensus, that if anyone didn't turn up for training on Tuesdays and Thursdays, they would automatically drop down to the next team. If a third team player did this (as there was no lesser team to drop down to), they would not be available for selection. After the usual arguments and discussion, this policy was adopted by all. It led to some rather unusual occurrences.

Football training on Tuesdays and Thursdays consisted of a five mile run approx through some of the streets and estates of Liverpool. It was before the floodlights were installed on the pitch and it was, therefore, in the dark. Consequently, the route (which varied from week to week) had to be well lit. Sadly, in the early seventies, no-one thought to tell the government, miners or the electric companies that we had training on these nights and we needed the street lights on. There were scheduled power cuts to save electricity and the coal stocks, as well as the usual ones. The supply of electricity was intermittent to say the least. We had managed to avoid the power cuts up to a point, until one fateful Thursday.

As usual, we set off on our run – about forty blokes in total. The quicker ones were at the front leading the way, whilst we slower runners would be bringing up the rear. I knew my place and this was near the rear! Whilst jogging steadily, my shoelace became undone and I bent down to do it up.

"Don't wait for me. I'll catch you up when I'm done."

As I was fastening my lace, all the lights went out. Power cuts had kicked in! My eyesight is not brilliant in the dark as I take quite a while to become adjusted to the light level. I quickly stood up and I could hear the cursing and swearing from the rest of the lads somewhere in the distance, so I set off in that direction. It really was pitch black and there was no moon visible as there was a large cloud cover. Tentatively, I jogged towards the noise and immediately fell off the kerb – I couldn't see a thing! Do I carry on or wait until my eyes became acclimatised to the dark? I carried on carefully and I was able to help myself as there was a wall on my right hand side. Suddenly the wall stopped and I could no longer hear the banter from ahead, so I slowed down almost to a walk. No car lights, no house lights and no street lights did not make for a safe passage. Jogging slowly forward, I suddenly hit something, waist high, did a complete somersault and a huge metal object fell on top of me as I hit the ground. After the usual curses, "Oh golly gosh! I appear to be pinned underneath a large motorcycle."

Yes, I had hit a 1000cc Yamasaki and it was now on top of me, pinning my arms to the ground. I couldn't move in any direction, I was completely stuck. The only good thing was I was only about half a mile from college and hopefully, someone would come and rescue me. As I lay there, for what seemed like hours, there were voices not too far away and they seemed to be coming closer. Suddenly a torch light appeared and I was blinded by the sudden light. Then gasps of astonishment as two figures hauled the Yamasaki off me and I scrambled to my feet a little dazed and slightly bruised but otherwise alright. My explanation caused raucous laughter from the bikers as they had not seen anything like it before. They were going in the same direction as me, so they kick started the bike, put the headlight on and drove very slowly, lighting my way. I arrived back at college and met up with the boys who were in the changing rooms in candlelight. They obviously thought I was just skiving off the run and really did not believe me when I told them the tale. However, I did have a few cuts and bruises to back up my story. A few beers went down well that night when the electricity came back on.

It was customary with the footy lads, that everyone would do something special on their twenty first birthday. Needless to say, it involved copious amounts of alcohol and usually some stupid behaviour which may or may not get the police involved. During these binges, it was especially pleasing to note that no-one got hurt, apart from a few cuts and bruises while falling over. It was up to the birthday boy to decide on the evenings activities and they ranged from the quiet pub night to the bizarre.

One summer day, we found out it was Dicko's birthday and this coincided with a Friday. Being education day, we were quite ready to be bored to tears during the day, in anticipation for the nightly activities. The usual homemade cards, with lots of boobs and bottoms, were given to Dicko during the day, in the hope of causing as much embarrassment as possible. A rousing chorus of Happy Birthday greeted him in the dining hall at break, together with a hammering on the table of cups, saucers and spoons etc. Then a short speech, "Thank you bastards!"

Dicko said to meet in the college bar at 6pm in order to move off at 7pm sharp. He added we should all wear smart casuals as the venue required suitable clothing. This set the tongues wagging. Where was he taking us? We couldn't wait and by 6pm we were all assembled in the college bar. The smell of Brut aftershave was overpowering and it was pleasing to note that we all looked quite respectable. Beer was consumed at a phenomenal rate and Dicko was thoroughly enjoying being the centre of attention. At 7pm a single decker coach rolled up and we all piled on ready for the night ahead. A tour of Liverpool's 'classier' pubs was planned, followed by a surprise! The coach pulled up at the first pub which was so classy, it had a wine bar. We'd never seen a wine bar in Liverpool before. However, once inside we did not look out of place and we started to enjoy the crazy cocktails, which were an excellent addition to the three pints of brown ale we'd had at college.

As the evening progressed, we were taken to three more classy pubs/wine bars and started to really get the hang of it. All too soon, however, the barman called 'TIME' and we had to finish our drinks. What was going to happen next? We piled into the coach and moved off. This time, we were heading for the more 'seedy' areas of Liverpool and the streets didn't look very inviting. Dicko got on the microphone and announced we were heading to "Dutch Eddy's". The bus went silent and people started speaking in hushed tones. The aforementioned hostelry was an afterhours drinking club in the 'black' section of Liverpool, near Upper Parliament Street. We had heard of Dutch Eddy's, but surely the rumours couldn't be true if we were on the way there. Apparently, Dicko had somehow met up with the doorman and had slipped him a few quid on the understanding we could come inside and savour the atmosphere. It was a place where many of the professional ladies and their pimps hung out and it had been the scene of many a shooting in the past. Just before we disembarked, Dicko came over the microphone, "Right, we're here. We'll have to make our own way home by cab, as the coach driver is not hangin' about in this area. Just a couple of words of warning! Look down. Don't make eye contact with anyone, not even the barman. Have a couple of drinks, but don't start chatting up the women unless they chat you up first. If anyone says you're sitting on their stool, politely apologise and then move. Be afraid, be very afraid. Other than that, have a good time."

As we climbed the few steps to the club, we were approached out of the shadows by a huge West Indian chap. He was dressed in a smart suit and had a voice like thunder,

"What you want?"

Dicko then had a few words with him and we were ushered in.

It was amazing how grand the foyer and cloakroom were, and when we went through into the blackness of the main room, it was difficult to see what it was really like. There were a few white faces amongst the clientele, but most were black. When our eyes became accustomed to the dark and smoke, it was clear that some of the pimps were in, as they were instantly recognisable in their yellow, pink or white suits and just like an American cameo, some were wearing fedoras and others large brimmed hats. We were actually shown to a group of tables and we ordered drinks, which surprisingly were reasonably priced. We were starting to relax a little and there was a combo playing jazz/funk in the opposite corner which was quite nice. Just when the drinks started to flow again, Dobbsy, from our group started chatting up a really pretty black girl wearing a silver dress, at the bar. After a few minutes, there was a movement at the front and two black guys were heading forcefully towards Dobbsy. Dicko, who was quite inebriated by now, saw them first and tried to 'head them off at the pass.' He just got there before the two guys arrived and cajoled Dobbsy away from the bar. The black guys were looking daggers at Dobbsy as Dicko just turned towards them and said,

"Sorry lads, this fella's a real nob 'ed," as he pointed to Dobbsy. Fortunately, this got a grin from the two black guys.

After a couple more drinks and chat, we were well sozzled and it was time to make a move, we had had enough scares and excitement for one night. We counted up in our semi comatose state and there was one guy missing.

"Has anyone seen Dicko? Has anyone checked the toilet?"

No sign of Dicko anywhere. Well, the consensus of opinion was that he could find his own way home as he was a big boy. We'd been hanging around for long enough and there was still no sign of him.

We said farewell to the gigantic doorman and hailed a few cabs to deliver us back to sanity. Where had the birthday boy gone?

No sign of Dicko at breakfast or at morning break. However, there was massive applause at lunchtime in the dining hall as Dicko appeared, white faced and not looking at all well.

"Where have you been birthday boy?"

"I really dunno what's goin' on!"

"What do you mean? How did you get home last night?"

"I didn't. I woke up in bed this morning, with this big black lady. I've no idea how I got there and was amazed when she wanted £20. I just threw on my kit and legged it. I'm late 'cos I've been down the pox clinic to get checked out!"

Fortunately, all was well in Dicko's nether regions.

As this was a mixed college with church associations, it was deemed essential that there should be no 'hanky panky' after midnight. Indeed, the porters/security chappies were very stringent in their patrols and took this separation of the sexes very seriously. The live-in students inhabited two separate wings of the main building accommodation, with males on one side and females on the other. Although they were joined by an upstairs corridor, this was very well lit at night and it was in direct sight of the porters' office. How on earth they thought that this would stop any sort of shenanigans, is beyond me. It was quite normal to see groups of males and females heading off in the 'wrong' direction after the bar closed, presumably to enjoy cups of coffee and each other's company. As the porters were not allowed on the female corridors, once people were ensconced in their rooms, they were not going to be shifted.

Usually, after a session in the bar, a number of us would retire to one of the girls' rooms and drink coffee and chat until the small hours. For the most part, nothing untoward happened and we often used to while away the hours playing a card game called 'sweaty Betty'. (I think the proper name was 'Chase the lady'.) Anyway, it involved the queen of spades as Betty and it soon became a nightly ritual (apart from weekends). Lots of laughter and fun ensued and it also became very competitive and a 'sweaty Betty' exercise book was procured in which to record the scores. Then sides were configured, usually lads against lasses. It was so much fun!

The problem came at 1- 2 in the morning, when the lads had to leave the premises and not get caught by the porters patrolling the grounds. To do this was no easy matter, as the study bedsits were on the first floor and we had to open a window at the end of the corridor and climb out holding on to the ledge, before dropping to the ground. Naturally, if we were spotted by the porters, we had to leg it. Usually, the porters gave chase for about thirty or forty yards, but as they were old geezers and we were in the prime of youth (albeit slightly inebriated), we usually gave them the slip. I only ever heard of one instance when someone got caught and that was because they were so drunk, they fell awkwardly and knocked themselves out. The youth in question was found underneath the window, still unconscious and still very drunk. He could not remember a thing that had happened, so the porter took him along to their office, plied him with tea and biscuits and then sent him on his way. All heart those guys.

It was after one of these sessions before midnight, that I dropped from a window in order to make my way back to my digs, which were almost a mile away. I cleared the wall of the college and was walking back when I met a group of three lads coming the other way. It was quite a well-lit road and there were frequent cars and taxis passing back and forth. I nodded as they approached and one of them asked, quite politely, for a light for his cigarette. One of the other guys asked how far it was to Broad Green and the third guy, who looked well gone on drink or other substances, pulled out what looked like a sharpened down chisel. The other two of his mates looked absolutely stunned! It was like slow motion, but it happened very quickly, he made a lunge at me. Instinct took over, as I felt this object touch my skin and I lashed out with my foot, catching him fair and square in the 'proverbials'. I didn't wait to see what happened as I legged it at speed down the road. The adrenalin had kicked in and it wasn't long before I reached my digs. I was so out of breath and so frightened that they were behind me that I couldn't get the key in the lock, so I just hammered on the door. Fortunately,

Ken and Kate, my landlords, were not in bed and came running when they heard the commotion.

As the door was opened, I fell in, still clutching my guts as I had done all the way home. There was a small amount of blood and Kate (who was a theatre sister) went into 'nursey' mode. I was laid down on the sofa in the lounge and my shirt was pulled up and my jeans down while she inspected the damage. Fortunately, any major injury was prevented by my leather belt, which had taken the brunt of the force and the skin had been cut just above the belt line. Ken was despatched to the bathroom dispensary and brought back miles of bandages, cotton wool and bottles of antiseptic etc. Kate, very delicately and professionally patched me up. Although it was just a superficial wound, I was obviously in shock. That's probably why Ken thrust a glass of brandy into my hand. Needless to say, he was forced to have one too! Kate very kindly pulled my jeans up and tucked my shirt in very gently over what seemed like a huge swathe of bandage. As I recounted the tale, another brandy was had by all and I was starting to feel quite relaxed. I had not had an in depth conversation with Ken and Kate before and it was nice to know them better, as another brandy was poured out. Kate had just finished her brandy when the conversation turned to football. At this point, Kate disappeared upstairs as another brandy was poured. Ken was a staunch Liverpool supporter and he was telling me all about the current Liverpool team, Callaghan, Clemence, Ian St. John etc and what was happening in the league. At about 2am we staggered up the stairs arm in arm singing 'You'll never walk alone' which he had kindly taught me.

There was no loud music from their room that night.

Occasionally we did some work at college none more so than when we went on field courses to various parts of the North West. Unfortunately, these short field courses happened during the first week of the holidays. There was one notable field course to Bangor on the Welsh Riviera. It was based at St. Mary's College, a teacher training college for ladies. It was a typical Victorian establishment, very traditional and very dour in some parts. It was atop a steep hill and overlooked the town, with not a pub in sight. Grey weathered stone and dark slate heralded our arrival in the monsoon season.

After unpacking and getting sorted into rooms and dorms etc., we made our way to the dining hall for lunch. In a magnificent dining hall, we were treated to a fabulous meal with silver cutlery which was stamped with "St Mary's College" and waitress service. Huge, immaculate chandeliers hung from the ceiling and there was a gallery all of the way round. We had never seen anything like it! On the top table was the Principal of the college, who fixed her steely glare on us as we arrived. Waitresses scuttled about on the top table, all bobbing and curtseying as well as 'yes ma'am-ing' all over the place. Our tutor and one or two other members of their staff, were well looked after there. Our waitresses were delightful and were quite happy to converse with us and by the end of our stay, were laughing and enjoying their lot.

After lunch, we congregated in a huge classroom area which had been set out with large tech drawing style boards and paper. We had brought a lot of equipment with us, but we were told that we needed some specialist items and these could be bought at an arty shop in town.

A few of us decided to go into town and purchase the said items, on the understanding that we had to be back in one hour. This didn't leave us much time to do the business, as the hill was very steep. Basically, the time limit was set so we did not have time to visit the local hostelries. We later found out that Brian Blogsworth (our tutor) was a Methodist and teetotaller, thoroughly against alcoholic beverages. Nevertheless, we legged it down to town, bought the equipment, found a pub, had a couple of pints, downed some strong mints to take the smell away and made our way back up the hill in just over the hour. Even Brian was impressed with our punctuality. The rest of the afternoon was spent organising the few day's events and planning who did what in our groups.

Soon it was time for dinner and off we went to the dining hall for another sumptuous meal. The Principal was already in situ and we wondered if she was a cardboard cut-out, as she sat very erect and hardly moved, except to give us the steely stare as we came in. The three course meal was magnificent and as there was no-one sat on the right of me, I decided to borrow the cutlery and popped them in my jeans pocket. We were all looking forward to our free time as Bangor looked OK from a pub point of view. However, we were directed back to the classroom, where we spent the next two hours, practising drawing graphs on large sheets of graph paper. When we asked Brian when we were having some free time, he just mumbled something about no time as we only had four days and not a week. It looked like we were going to be working until about 10pm every night! We were not amused.

After a sober evening, we completed our ablutions in the morning and went down for a magnificent cooked breakfast. The Principal was still in situ – presumably she had been there all night. Soon we were piled on to our mini buses and on the road towards Anglesey across the fantastic Menai Bridge. The scenery was breathtaking as we passed across the island and headed towards our base camp on the beach at Trearddur Bay. We quickly unloaded our equipment and Brian pitched a little tent to store the essentials, should it rain. The weather was glorious as the monsoon had abated and we quickly set about our tasks in our set groups. Measuring the slope of the beach, identifying seaweeds, measuring the position and the angle of apex of limpet shells, how much more excitement could we take?

The day remained beautiful and the beach was sandy for the most part and rocky at one end which was handy for our limpet survey. Packed lunch was a revelation, with smoked salmon and other goodies. It was such a shame to pack up at about 6pm, as even the hardened dossers had enjoyed it so much. So after the drive back to St. Mary's and the sprucing up, we were all looking forward to our sumptuous dinner and even more to our free time at the pub. Dinner was the usual high standard and the cardboard cut-out of the Principal was still there, with the usual steely eyes. After dinner we were told to relax in the common room and enjoy a coffee, which we duly did. At this point, Brian came in and informed us that we were to go to the classroom and draw massive charts and graphs, as well as catalogue the samples we had brought back. We were astonished. It was Friday night and it was customary to imbibe a little alcoholic refreshment, we were students, after all.

But no! Our noses were kept to the grindstone until about 10pm when it was time for bed. To our astonishment, the same procedure occurred on Saturday. This was just not cricket. No beverages on Thursday, Friday or Saturday. What had the world come to?

Sunday dawned and after a short survey in the morning, we were told to pick up our packed lunches and then we were free to wander around Bangor to buy any souvenirs and maybe have a coffee. Just as we were about to set off, Brian announced, "Oh by the way. It's Sunday. As this is a 'dry' county, it means that the pubs are not open."

This was a ritual in some Welsh counties that the pubs stay shut on Sundays. We then asked a colleague, Phil, who was Welsh and he confirmed that Bangor was indeed 'dry' on Sundays. With a little pressure, we asked him to come up with a solution as no shops would sell alcohol either. After much thought, he asked an old chap who was sat outside his front door, where we could get a drink on a Sunday. With a huge grin on his face, he told us to go round the corner for about a hundred yards and we would see a white building which would look shut but it wasn't. Knock on the double doors and when someone answers, tell them that 'Bryn the milk' had sent you along.

After wishing us well and shaking our hands, the dirty dozen did exactly as we were told and after giving the gentleman the passwords, we were ushered into the RAOB club after a small donation was made to the funds. Inside, it was fantastic. Seats, tables and lots of blokes and a few ladies swilling beer as quickly as I've ever seen it swilled outside of the college bar. We were welcomed again by pleasant people and we ordered a round of drinks. As we sat down at a couple of tables, not much was said at first as we were terribly thirsty. The first two pints went down like lightening and were quickly replenished. It was really nice to chat to some locals who managed to scrounge a few beers from us. After about six or seven pints, it was just about time to wend our way back to the minibuses. One or two of us were a little unsteady on our feet and indeed were talking rather loudly and slurring words.

When Brian caught sight of us, he went berserk. He could not believe we had managed to obtain large quantities of alcohol on a Sunday in a dry county.

"Never in all my life have I seen so much alcohol abuse. This cannot be tolerated. I will pray for you all."

Now, considering Brian had never been in the college bar, he wouldn't have seen alcohol abuse on this scale. This was just the normal chain of events for a student and we wondered where and how he had spent his University days.

The way back to our college was in silence. Most of us had fallen asleep anyway and Brian was determined not to talk to any of us because of the shenanigans. That fella really had a lot to learn.

Whilst at college, I was privileged to play for a local tennis team. While it was not Wimbledon standard, it was quite exciting and very enjoyable. We also got to travel to other establishments and to sample beer from all over the Liverpool area. It was a general rule that the home team provided a 'tea' for everyone who played in the matches. This was usually followed by a lengthy stint in the bar afterwards and apart from the driver, it usually meant we all had a skinful. It was good visiting these other clubs and it was made even better by the fact that the beer was really cheap.

During one of these outings we met a guy called Bob Johnson, who played for a rival club. Bob Johnson was not his real name, as his name given at birth was just too complicated and difficult to pronounce. Bob was a jet black Nigerian, the son of a tribal chief who had been sent to England with the hope of furthering his education and playing tennis, which was his favourite sport. When he arrived in this country he was very naive but being in Liverpool, he quickly learned the ways of the world. He had studied hard to become a teacher and was now teaching PE and games in one of the local comprehensives. We got on really well whenever we played Bob's team and he enthralled us with some amazing stories, mainly about his sexual prowess.

After one really close-fought tennis match, the bar beckoned and we sat down with Bob and a couple of the opposition. Our initial discussions were about tennis and soon we were all saying how we would like to do our coaching certificates. I said I would look into this and see if there were any classes which we could attend. They all left their names and contact numbers and we proceeded then to drink the bar dry. After a few days, I found a centre and signed everyone up to start as soon as possible. The course was quite tough. It lasted for one evening a week over about twelve weeks and at the end, there was a practical exam at the local school and a written exam. We all threw our heart and soul into these lessons and soon it was time for the exam. We turned up in our newly washed and pressed whites, sat the written paper and were called out one at a time to do the practical assessment. After this we had to go back and finish the written exam, it was quite gruelling.

When we had finished the exam, we were all exhausted and clambering for a beer or three. We all piled into a couple of cars and as Bob knew of a little country pub just on the outskirts of Liverpool, we followed the lead car to the little country pub. On our arrival, we looked around the car park and it was full of 'Beamers', 'Mercs' and 'Jags'. Had we come to the wrong pub? Bob assured us we had not, although it was a couple of years since he had been. It looked as though it had had a makeover during that time.

I was not looking forward to this somehow, especially as Bob leapt out of the car in his pristine whites wearing a white tea cosy hat. His white teeth were somehow illuminated in the blackness as we approached the large double oak door. What was waiting behind the door was definitely not 'ye old fashioned country pub'. As Bob thrust open the double doors and strode in, we were amazed to see a large well lit bar straight ahead of us and lots of small tables with dimmed table lights and couples drinking G & Ts, Campari, etc and tête-à-tête-ing across the table. Undaunted, Bob strode in complete with his white tea cosy hat and his teeth glistening. As he approached the bar, with us in tow, there was a very bored looking barman, looking at the ceiling, polishing wine glasses. Bob strode on and in a loud voice which dwarfed the piped music blurted out,

"Hey man! Give me a beer and a crocodile and coconut sandwich."

Without altering his gaze or halting his polishing, he replied,

"I'm sorry sir, we've just run out of bread!"

Needless to say, the place erupted in laughter.

Inevitably, at the end of each academic year looms the auspicious 'Exam Week', where almost every student goes into meltdown. Our college was not an exception and it was a time for the real dossers to show their true colours, to swot or not to swot? That is the question. In the majority of cases it meant that programmes of revision were set about a week before the final exams, except for the knitting circle who had been diligently cramming for weeks. During the final week before exams, "DO NOT DISTURB" notices were hung on doors from the late afternoon to the mid-evening. In fact some of these notices were hung on the doors very late in the evening, when extra-curricular activities used to take place. Most students had a set way of revising. Some liked peace and quiet, others liked a little background music to help them take in the vast quantities of knowledge that should have been imbibed during the year. Some had rather an eccentric method of revising and learning; one student used to walk the corridors, up and down, whilst reading from files and textbooks. He would constantly recite and mumble his way from one level to the next. Another student found she could absorb much of the education curriculum by knitting in a particular rhythm. One student in particular spent much of his revision time sat on the toilet with his files and books on his lap. This caused constant hilarity, as he would disappear into the toilet at about 2pm and emerge at about 6.30pm just in time for the evening meal. One afternoon, he was ensconced in his usual position on the loo, and we decided that if he liked the loo so much, perhaps he would like to spend longer in there. Someone produced a climbing rope, tied it around the door handle and then tied the other end to the metal railings on the stair well. We then went for our evening meal and totally forgot about 'Drew locked in the loo'. After we had eaten, someone suggested a quick pint and as there were no objectors, we all trundled into the bar for refreshment. At about 8.30pm we emerged and went up to our rooms to do some work, a rare occurrence! Just as we were approaching the study rooms' corridor, we heard the banging and the muffled curses. We had totally forgotten about Drew in the loo. We rushed round and untied the door. Drew had missed his evening meal and had been in the loo for about six hours. He was not amused. After exams, the atmosphere was mental. The bar takings went up 400% and there was lots of new (and old) liaisons taking place. Exam week was forgotten and everyone was looking forward to the holidays or in most cases, working to earn enough money to keep them in beer and fags for the next term. There was a 'Rag Week' where lots of the students did stupid things to raise cash for a local charity. Comedy performances were written, rehearsed and performed for the rest of college and to their credit, many of the staff attended too. For the intellectuals, a lecturer played six games of chess simultaneously, blindfold (without seeing the boards, he sat behind a large screen and he drank quite a few brown ales). The culmination of all these activities was the 'Going down Ball' on the Saturday night.

It was almost surreal to see these unkempt, smelly footy lads turned out so wonderfully in their DJs, with a beautiful young lady on their arm. Photos were taken in the foyer on entry and the hall was done out beautifully with lots of balloons and tinsel and large decorations.

Usually, a half famous band appeared live and in-between sets there was a professional DJ making good music. The bar was massive and there were barrels of beer in reserve. Everyone was served with champers and canapés on entry and the evening was always a knockout.

One of these balls, which I attended, had The Tremeloes playing live and whilst their music was not to everyone's taste, it did not matter. They were very professional and the sound quality was fantastic. The wine and beer was flowing and it was such an exceptional night. Everyone was dancing with everyone else, even boys with boys! The knitting circle had finally let their hair down and the girls were joining in the fun and games. Unfortunately, it came to an end all too soon and as we trooped out arm in arm with our partners, a lone piper stood on a balcony just outside the hall, a spotlight capturing his glory as he played Amazing Grace. The tears flowed and everyone stopped to listen just as it started to drizzle. After he had finished, there was thunderous applause from the gathered throng. Our life at college was over, well not quite; there was a relaxed atmosphere as the gentlemen escorted the ladies back to their rooms for coffee and afters. The porters were nowhere in sight, probably having their own celebrations for the end of the academic year. The footy lads had one final prank up their sleeves. There was a strange request to the ladies for a number of bras. Six were collected and tied end to end. A few lunatics then climbed up the bell tower and raised the six bras to the top of the flagpole, where they gently fluttered in the breeze. The flagpole rope was then tied in a position that could not be reached without the aid of ladders. How long they remained there is anyone's guess. We left college later that morning when the sun had risen.

Chapter 4

Holidays

1-The Manchester Nutter (and other Spanish adventures)

Lloret de Mar! This name sent tears of joy to all the drunks and reprobates in the early seventies. It was the Ayia Napa of its time and was a perfect venue for eight male college students, let out on the razzle in the summer holidays. After working all the summer holidays to fund this escapade, it was now time to spend lots of potatas (pesetas) drinking the likes of cava, Bacardi and watery beer and trying to impress as many ladies as possible. The hotel was booked (or so we thought), the flight to Alicante was arranged, as was the transport to Luton airport and to the hotel Bella Vista. The day before we were due to leave, we were told that the hotel had overbooked and that two of our party would have to stay in another hotel at the other side of town. Obviously, we could do nothing about this and it was quickly decided that 'Tee' and 'Bob' would stay in the alternative accommodation. We later found out that they had been upgraded to 'all inclusive' and the hotel was classified as 5* compared to our 4*. The scene was set for the greatest amount of shenanigans since the previous holiday.

Day 1

The flight and transfer were without any major incident, except one of our group, (Tim), was terrified of flying. We did not find this out until we had parked the hire car and were entering the airport terminal to check in. After checking in, we made our way through to the main part of the terminal, via duty free, where booze and ciggies were purchased with gay abandon. At this point, we lost Tim. We scoured the terminal, but we couldn't find him anywhere. After a twenty minute search, Tim was spotted at the back of a bar downing his third double Bacardi and coke. Nothing unusual in this apart from the fact it was 6.30 am and Tim was a definite 'lightweight' when it came to alcohol intake. He muttered an apology and as he ordered his fourth double, he told us of his fear of flying. After the initial flak he got for this, we all decided to join him in his fear and we too ordered double Bacardi's to appease our nerves.

As our flight was called for boarding, we placed sunglasses on Tim and 'helped' him through the gate and onto the plane. Fortunately, there was a slight delay for take-off and during this time, Tim fell fast asleep. In fact he was probably unconscious, but at least it got him through the flight.

Passport control was a laugh, as we helped Tim through. The passport guy was so nonplussed seeing Tim being 'guided' by his mates. He seemed to come round very quickly as we collected our baggage and piled on the coach to our destination. There were lots of nice couples of all ages staying at our hotel who were allocated rooms from the first to the fifth floor. We were allocated rooms on the seventh floor, together with quite a few other 'youngsters'. It was later discovered that the sixth floor was a 'no man's land' or a 'battle free zone' to separate the loonies above and the sane and sensible below. Hotel Bella Vista obviously had experience with youngsters out to have a good time and those on the normal family holiday.

Once we had unpacked, we headed off down the road to purchase some supplies. A friend had told us that the Spar shop down the road sold good quality cava for about a quarter of the price at our hotel. Our first purchase of 48 bottles emptied the shelves and we asked to borrow a wheelie trolley to transport it up the hill to our hotel. The manager was OK with this, but asked for a large deposit on the chariot which would be refunded on its return.

After drinking a bottle of cava each before dinner, we then had another bottle each, before heading off into town to view the sights. Tim seemed to have recovered from his earlier 'sickness' and he started to get into the swing of things by downing his share of the cava with aplomb.

Our first evening was spent touring the local watering holes, sussing out the best places for the ladies and the cheapest booze. Quite a few bars were noted and we befriended a number of bar staff, who supplied us with very large measures after a suitable tip. Tee and Bob joined us at one of these bars and it was then we discovered about the upgrade and their fantastic hotel. So our first night/morning was coming to an end and after saying our good byes to Tee and Bob (who headed back to their luxurious accommodation), we made it back to our hovel at about 3am.

Making our way to the 7th floor, we quickly climbed into our pits and fell asleep almost at once. We were awakened from our slumbers at about 4am with a loud crash followed about 30 seconds later by shouting and other noises, mainly in Spanish. It soon quietened down and we did not bother to find out what was going on. We were sure all would be revealed in the morning.

Day 2

Arising early (just before midday) to bright sunshine was a little disconcerting, as we had driven to Luton the previous, night in steady rain. Blinds were opened sheepishly and showers were in full swing a few minutes later, as six doe-eyed students emerged for lunch. Copious quantities of water were drunk during lunch before heading off to the pool for even more sleep. At about 4pm, the first cocktail was ordered. As we had never had cocktails before, it was quite an experience! After bribing the waiter with a couple of packets of English ciggies, we settled down to a few more free cocktails. Afternoon turned to evening and we all disappeared to our rooms to imbibe the customary 2 bottles of cava before heading out for the evening entertainment. Calling in at the usual bars for our free drinks, courtesy of our bribed barmen, we partied hard, and had a small amount of luck with the ladies. Four of us seemed to score, with a promise to meet up the following evening. As we were still quite tired and a little tiddly, we made our way back to our hotel. No sign of Tee and Bob!

Day 3

At about 4am, we were awakened again by another loud crash and some loud shouting in Spanish again. This time all six of us poked our heads outside our doors. It appeared that the management and security guard were having a frantic argument with a 5' 2" Mexican bloke, with the biggest sombrero and biggest black moustache I have ever seen. We were ushered back into our rooms and the hullabaloo quietened down. We didn't quite make it for breakfast, but as we took our places by the pool, we noticed a sunbed with a large sombrero covering a small person. This person remained in this state for about another four hours, before emerging at about 3pm. Lo and behold, it was the Mexican chap from the previous night. Tim was the only guy amongst us to speak Spanish and so he was despatched to find out what had gone on the previous night. Discovering that this Mexican was in fact English, he was asked to join us for the customary 'sundowner'

It appears he was from Manchester and was a tax inspector. He had a boring 9-5 job for fifty weeks of the year and for two weeks every year, he let out all his frustrations abroad. At home he hardly drank alcohol, but while on holiday he endeavoured to give himself chronic liver damage by drinking anything and everything. Each morning at 4am, he would arrive back at the hotel, get the lift to his room and then throw his suitcase through the French windows in his room. When asked why he had not been arrested or thrown out of the hotel, he would mention to the hotel management that he would smash all the windows on the ground floor of the hotel and this apparently seemed to pacify them! I had never heard anything like it

That evening, after our usual aperitifs and digestifs, we made our way out for the now customary riotous evening. Wending our way back to our hotel at about 3am, we couldn't wait for the usual fiasco at 4am. We struggled to stay awake, but at about 3.55am we heard the gentle hum of the lift climbing to the seventh floor. This was followed by a gentle 'ping' as the lift reached its destination, followed quickly by the noise of the doors opening. Then…

"Aye yi yi yi! Charlton is better than Pele".

Bang! As the door was kicked in.

Crash! As the suitcase flew out through the French windows and on to the balcony.

Gabbling of Spanish voices and some new voices, which we later discovered were two police officers. The Manchester nutter was to spend the night in a Spanish gaol and we could all get some sleep

Day 4

The following morning, we all made it down for breakfast, which consisted of fruit juice, coffee, fruit juice, fruit juice and coffee. After this magnificent appearance at breakfast, which totally shocked the waiters who had no idea who we were, we then retired to the pool area where we were greeted with thunderous applause as we had never once made it before the afternoon. We had made a lot of good friends, especially with the waiters, who had supplemented their meagre income with loads of bribe money to supply us with as much drink as we could handle. So funnily enough, at about 10.30 am (a record for this holiday, which stood the test of time!), the first cocktails appeared. Manuel (it had to be didn't it...) was duly primed to keep these appearing every half an hour, with a few extra potatas bribe money. With six thirsty students to attend to and the promise of more potatas, we were his prime customers and he kept the booze flowing nicely. Drinking between snoozes or snoozing between drinks was a splendid way to pass a morning. It was getting close to lunch, when great excitement ensued.

Tee and Bob, who had not been seen for a couple of days, duly arrived on hired bicycles. They had picked them up right outside their hotel and had bartered hard to get these for a week. They had duly cycled over to our hotel, whereupon they had ridden up the side of the hotel, around the back, up the ramp and rode them straight into the swimming pool. More thunderous applause followed, and more drinks were obtained from Manuel. In fact, this was such a great event, that four bottles of cava appeared on our table from a grateful pool population. This seemed to have the desired magnetic effect on the available female population as well, and before long we were regaling them with tales of derring-do and plying them with alcohol in the hope of having our evil way! One young lady in particular seemed to get a lot of attention, not because of her good looks as she was quite plain, but because of her tanned statuesque figure, which seemed to have considerable bumps in all the right places. Consequently, she was nicknamed "La Boda" (the body). Everyone tried their hardest to impress La Boda, but she remained unattached to any particular person, just determined to have a good time. She certainly did that, as she downed vast quantities of alcohol and her body just looked better and better.

After lunch, the temperature hit 32+ and it was soon time for the afternoon nap before the evening festivities started. We awoke at about 4pm to the sound of a siren and paramedics running up the ramp (now called the "Tee & Bob landing strip"). What had happened? An old geezer (about 40 years old) had fallen asleep without any sun cream and was now crying with pain. So much so, it looked as though he had suffered a stroke or heart attack and he was whisked away on a stretcher by the paramedics. Wow! Such excitement! It was not to end there... An impromptu human pyramid was started by the deep end of the pool. We almost had sufficient numbers to complete it ourselves, but we were lucky that some of our new friends helped us out, with La Boda completing the 4, 3, 2, 1 pyramid at the top. We held it together for about a minute, just long enough for the pool crowd to take photographs and then we all fell in the deep end, a splendid end to a splendid afternoon. Soon it would be time for the evening meal and the start of the evening entertainment. What a surprise we had in the dining room as we sat down for our evening meal In walked the Manchester nutter, wearing a blue Mexican hat with a metre wingspan, a multi-coloured poncho and a plastic child's guitar slung round his neck. He proceeded to give a good rendition of "O solo mio", whilst strumming away on the plastic guitar. Naturally, thunderous applause greeted this fabulous singing and he started serenading every female in the dining room, often getting down on bended knee. After about five minutes, he finished the song and the rapturous applause could have been heard in town. He had spent the night in a police cell and threatened with deportation if the 4am fiasco continued. As it was only day four of his fortnight holiday, he had agreed to moderate his behaviour and not to cause any more damage at the hotel. However, things were to take a turn for the worse after dinner. He approached our table and in the most cheesy, gruff Mexican voice ever, he said to me, "Hey gringo! You and me will have some beers tonight."

Bearing in mind that this nutter was capable of anything, I stupidly agreed. He was invited into the inner sanctum of the cava room for the customary topping up of blood/alcohol levels, and then the two of us made our way to the first port of call, The White Horse pub. He seemed quite quiet and reserved, but still persevered in this stupid Mexican accent. All seemed quite normal in the pub with the usual array of drunks already getting their acts together, so we sat down quietly in the corner and had a nice cool beer. The nutter removed his hat, probably for the first time that day, although no-one had seen him before dinner. The conversation flowed quite amicably and he told me that he came on holiday by himself as none of his mates would dare to. Quite sad really!

As the evening progressed, one or two of the local drunks decided to dance on the tables to the crappy piped disco music. Perhaps this was just what the nutter was waiting for, as it was like a red rag to a bull. Immediately the hat was back on and within a few seconds, he too was on the table. Not content with a samba/salsa/rumba however, he lifted up three chairs and stacked them one on top of another. Then he proceeded to climb these as the clapping and cheering got louder and louder. Finally (and miraculously) he reached the top of this column and stood in triumph with his arms in the air. His hands touched the rafters on the ceiling and there was a solid iron bar which connected the rafters to the wall. He grabbed this and swung in time to the music and the clapping of the assembled throng. When the music stopped, the cheering and the applause were deafening. At this point the manager came over and asked him to get down. However, he insisted that he couldn't! His arm had gone into some sort of spasm and he said he couldn't let go. Everyone thought he was joking, but reality set in when we realised he had been hanging there one handed for the best part of ten minutes. Eventually, a barman brought some tall step ladders and positioned them under the nutter, delicately climbing them and gently prising apart his grip on the iron bar. He was then lowered carefully into the arms of the local drunks to even louder applause than before. After taking a bow we then moved on to a quiet bar on the front, next to the promenade. I'd had enough excitement for one evening. It just could not get any worse; we each had a beer and a short, as both our nerves were shattered. The nutter seemed very apologetic and contrite. Our conversation inevitably turned to footy and girls. After a couple more beers, we were getting on fine and both of us seemed just a wee bit tipsy. All of a sudden, there was a very loud roar of engines from just outside the bar. It appeared that two Guardia (Franco's personal guards), were cruising slowly along the promenade, showing off their Harley

Davidsons with their sub machine guns around their shoulders. The crowds on the prom scattered to the side and gazed in awe at these two stormtroopers. Once again this seemed to act as a lit firework for the nutter, as he jumped off his bar stool, grabbed a bottle and ran out of the bar. The Guardia had just passed the bar and were about twenty metres further up the prom, when the nutter charged down the bar steps and into the centre of the empty prom, yelling and screaming at the top of his voice.

"F**k off you fascist bastards!

Tell Franco he is a little twat and should have his balls cut off and stuffed down his throat!"

Then he threw the bottle, which landed just between the two Harleys. Then the insults followed again together with a multitude of V signs with both hands.

I witnessed all of this from the relative safety of the bar window.

The two Guardia chappies calmly got off their bikes and casually kicked them onto their stands. With equal calm, they unshouldered their sub machine guns and aimed them in the direction of the nutter. It was at this point that the insults finally stopped and self-preservation started to kick in! The nutter ran towards the prom wall as about twenty rounds were fired in quick succession, pinging off and lighting up the top of the prom wall, he cleared the wall in one bound and disappeared onto the beach. This was some feat for such a small man, but the adrenalin rush must have been colossal, coupled with the vast quantities of alcohol, anything could have happened and it did.

We never saw the nutter again and still no sign of Tee and Bob.

Day 5

We had settled nicely into a routine at our hotel and we were all well known for our antics around the pool and in the dining room. Funnily enough, everyone seemed much more relaxed after the disappearance of the nutter and there was much more sun bathing and pool chat. Various relationships were starting to develop between the drunks and the girlies, which was nice. There was no pressure to start a meaningful relationship, so consequently there was a reasonable amount of bonking going on. Us lads had an arrangement, that if anyone had scored and wanted a little privacy, the bedroom was the domain of the partners and the other incumbent spent the night on a mattress in someone else's room. Various liaisons took place, but no-one managed a fling with La Boda.

Supplies of cava had run out and so we made an expedition into town to the Spar shop. Naturally, we were welcomed with open arms by the manager and as we loaded up our chariot, we were not asked for a massive deposit, as we were deemed trustworthy by the manager. This was excellent news and very welcome as we cleared the shelves of cava once again. The manager was delighted, but asked if we could give him notice when we required extra supplies. Of course we agreed and as a thank you, we were presented with a couple of extra bottles of cava and some cheap Bacardi.

Naturally, we arrived back at the hotel and after stashing the cava in the 'cava bedroom', we popped down to the pool with our litre bottle of Bacardi. We became everyone's friends as we supplied free Bacardi to friends and acquaintances. As this was such a success and gave us the opportunity of meeting new girlies, we decided to have a 'sundowner' on a regular basis. As promised, we notified the local Spar manager and bought ten bottles of Bacardi the following day. Naturally, with such courteous Brits, he threw in a couple of free bottles as well. The 'cava room' was getting quite full! We appointed Pietro Mann, the quietest member of our group, to maintain supplies of cava and Bacardi. He was very happy to undertake this responsibility and after the usual cava intake, we all disappeared into town with our entourage to dance the night away. Still no sign of Tee and Bob.

Day 6

Now what is Spain famous for (apart from sun, sea, sand, sex and sangria)? Bullfighting of course! We had no alternative, therefore, but to book ourselves in on a course to learn bullfighting at the local stadium. We were due to be picked up from the hotel at 2pm, so copious quantities of cava were drunk, as this could be quite an ordeal. Six semi paralytic English youths in a bullring could lead to all sorts of scenarios. We were extremely pleased to see that we were not the only ones who needed Dutch courage, as most people on the coach were well on the way to a comatose state.

We arrived at about 3pm, after collecting quite a few more drunks from other hotels and were then ushered into a small area with staged seating and barriers surrounding an oval space about half the size of a football pitch. The barriers were solid wood and were obviously in place to protect the small crowd from a rampaging bull. We took our seats until the stadium was about half full. Then a rather chunky Spaniard came out towards the centre of the 'ring' carrying a microphone. In a gravelly voice that was probably caused by heavy smoking, he started the proceedings....

"*Buenos tardes señores.* 'Ow are you tooday? My name is Pedro and I weel be your teesher to teesh you 'ow to fight the bull. I weel show you all ze moves and some of you weel practees what I teech you and I weel be the bull for your practees."

Phew, that sounded OK as we all had had visions of being charged at by a two ton monster. Pedro started his tuition and to be fair, he was very good, telling us how to hold the cape in front, before sidestepping at the last moment and swishing the cape over the bull. Looked easy enough!

"Now I want some people to 'ave a go! I weel be the bull."

He held his hands on his head with two pointed index fingers to represent horns and ran around with his head down. A very impressive bull we thought. Before we could say anything, our friend Johnny had vaulted the wooden barrier and was already on his way to the centre of the ring. Loud applause and the customary "Ole's" rang out.

Johnny held the cape and did remarkably well against 'Pedro the bull'. The other 'contestants' (who were as stupid as Johnny) did equally well. Then Pedro asked all the 'contestants' to take a place behind the barrier while he showed them how to fight a real bull. They duly climbed the barrier and peeped over to watch Pedro fight the bull!

The bull was released from the cage over the far side and it must have been about six months old as it ran into the ring. It had no horns whatsoever and ran over to Pedro like a long lost friend. Pedro was ready and he had his red cape, which he waved in front of the bull(ock). It seemed reluctant to do anything at first, but with the encouragement of the crowd and Pedro giving it a good talking to, it finally ran at the red cape. Pedro delicately sidestepped and dragged the cape over the bull(ock)'s head to great applause and shouts of "OLE!" from the spectators. The bull(ock) seemed to enjoy this and ran at Pedro a few times. Although Pedro was a portly gent, he was quite nimble on his feet and sidestepped the charges of the bull with great aplomb. Eventually, the bull(ock) got bored with this and eventually ran back to the cage at the other side of the ring.

"Now eet is your turn," said Pedro over the microphone. "Ooo wants to be the first to fight the leetle booll's brother?"

Over the fence went Johnny to shouts of "OLE! OLE!" and rapturous applause. After a few last minute instructions by Pedro and the doffing of his black furry hat to the crowd in every direction, he was ready for the entrance of the bull(ock)'s brother. Johnny took his place in the centre of the ring as the cage was opened, then nothing. As Johnny advanced toward the cage, there was a clang and a two ton, snorting angry animal, the size of a small caravan, with horns about a metre long, came hurtling out of the cage at phenomenal speed straight towards Johnny. After a split second of contemplation, the adrenalin kicked in and Johnny ran towards the wood barrier with the monster closing in fast. Johnny vaulted the wood barrier in one go and this was followed a second later by a massive thud as the horns of the Kraken smashed into the barrier. Johnny didn't hear the applause and the OLEs as he was still running in between the tiered seating towards the back exit. Various 'matadors' had appeared in the ring and were coaxing the Kraken back into its pen. Johnny was still cowering behind the seating when we all appeared after some more fun and games in the ring. Elf n Safety, eat your heart out.

After this excitement, Johnny was definitely in need of a drink and fortunately we were whisked away on the bus for a barbecue at this large finca in the middle of nowhere. Johnny had calmed down and was starting to feel OK after his third Bacardi and coke. We were seated at a large wooden table for about twelve, and a couple of blokes and some really nice girlies were ushered to our table as well. They recognised Johnny immediately and he quickly forgot his traumatic experience as he became the centre of attention. My friend Tim sat opposite me and we were delighted when two of the girlies came and sat next to us. Tim's girlie friend was very attractive and very talkative. However, the young lady next to me was also very attractive, but had the most horrendous stutter. After about fifteen minutes, I found out that she was from St. Helens. I had to be very patient to get any information out of her, and that was probably why her companion talked incessantly. However, after a few drinks, she became more lucid (or maybe the time passed more quickly in between stutters). The sangria flowed incessantly and the food was good; we were so hungry by this time, we would have eaten anything.

The compulsory drunken dancing ensued and everyone piled onto the dance floor for the silly pop dances that the Spanish are so good at. Why Spain has not won Eurovision more than once is beyond belief, as these 'clappy trappy' songs with actions were so bad. Eventually, the evening/early morning was drawing to a close and it was pleasing to notice that all of the boys had duly made the acquaintance of a lovely lady, and we all fell asleep in each other's arms on the coach back to town. The St. Helens stutterer was now in full swing and it was quite amazing how I found out that alcohol can cure the worst stutter on the planet! We arranged to meet all the girlies at their hotel the following evening and what a coincidence, not only were they staying at the same hotel as Tee and Bob, but they knew them both. With a last peck on the cheek, we said our goodbyes and we left them as we made our way back to our pits. Roll on tomorrow.

Day 7

Day seven dawned as many of the others did – in the afternoon. Lunch was taken followed quickly by the pool cocktails around our sunbeds. There was an air of quiet for a short spell as two of the elder people we had befriended were departing that afternoon. Sam and Dave, who were in their late forties, had joined in the silly antics and banter around the pool wholeheartedly and could cope with the oceans of sangria, cocktails and cava that was thrust upon them. Just before they left, Dave gave quite an emotional speech to the assembled throng, saying he and Samantha had never enjoyed a holiday so much. He also said they had left something to say thank you and hoped this would help us to remember them. He did not say what it was. After much kissing and handshakes, they made their escape from the pool crowd. Twenty minutes later, a very large cake appeared with a massive sparkler stuck in the top. In the icing on the top it just said "Thank you". A lovely gesture from two really nice people! Coupled with this was six bottles of cava, no doubt one for each of us. We were all very touched.

That evening after dinner and after the customary cava, the six hooligans made our way over to Tee and Bob's hotel, partly to see what they had been up to and partly to see the girlies we had met last night. We duly arrived at the 'Mediterranean Palace' and were stunned by the luxury of it all. There was a red carpet up the two or three steps and a doorman in a proper uniform who promptly stopped us and asked what we wanted in perfect English. We explained that we had been invited to join our friends in the cocktail lounge. We described our two friends and without a flicker of emotion, he said, "Ah, you mean Tee and Bob, two really nice gentlemen."

Now this didn't sound like our two friends. What had been going on?

The doorman kindly directed us into the cocktail bar, where we quietly sat and ordered some cocktails at scandalous prices and waited patiently for Tee and Bob or the girlies to appear.

On our way over to the 'Palace', we had called in at the local market, which was still revving at 9pm and we had had a good look round. There were all kinds of souvenirs and bric-a-brac, mostly aimed at the British holidaymaker. In one particular shop, we came across 'spud guns', which we hadn't seen for many a year. On the spur of the moment, we bought one each and also scrounged a potato for ammunition. The vendor was very accommodating in this respect. I noticed as well the biggest sombrero I had ever seen, over a metre wingspan, with a very tall central point. I thought I might purchase one of these on a later occasion and stored the info in my memory banks for later.

In the cocktail bar were a number of refined folk, gently sipping their 'tequila sunrises' and their 'sex on the beaches'. At the bar on beautiful bar stools were two stunning young ladies dressed in similar 'little black numbers' and showing a vast amount of tanned thigh and cleavage. Wow! We had never seen anything as refined as this before, and no-one made a move as this was a new situation. Normally, we would have swooped on them and plied them with copious quantities of cheap booze, in the hope of having our evil way. But we just sat in silence as we stared…

The coma was broken when in walked Tee and Bob, looking very dapper. Great frivolity ensued and another round of expensive cocktails was ordered. After the initial greetings and questions about where they had been, the topic turned to the two girls at the bar. Apparently, Tee and Bob had been trying to chat them up since they arrived at the hotel, but with no luck whatsoever. Tee said, "Ah, I see you have seen the International Jet Set then. That's the reason why we have been absent from the fun and games over at your place."

"Have you had any luck in your ventures?" said Simon.

"Not a dickie bird," said Bob. "They just ignore us!"

Docker said, "I bet we can get a reaction out of them. They won't ignore us."

"OK," said Tee. "If you can get a reaction out of them, we'll buy the drinks all night."

This was agreed.

"OK lads. Load your weapons" as six spud guns were armed.

"Take aim! Fire!"

Six spud guns were fired across the posh cocktail bar and one (or two) hit a delicate glass held by one of the International Jet Set as she was about to take a sip. The contents were emptied over one black little number, all the way down the front!

The foul mouthed language and torrent of abuse that emanated from that refined lady, even shocked some of us as well as the other wine bar connoisseurs.

Naturally, the commotion was heard by the doorman, who entered all of a fluster and promptly asked us and the young ladies to leave. The stream of abuse continued as we were ejected from the building, and the girls went to their room to change, presumably into another little black number. Tee and Bob apologised profusely to the doorman and the cocktail bar staff and gave the excuse that they didn't really know us, we had just had a drink together on the plane. Well we certainly got a reaction.

Looks like the drinks would be on Tee and Bob that night.

As we stood by the door of the hotel, the two girlies who we had befriended and some others appeared, as they had heard the commotion from the other bar. We all had hugs and kisses (apart from Tee and Bob, who had been wasting valuable pick up time trying to chat up the International Jet Set), and merrily set off into town for our usual fun and games. Six of us linked arms with girlies and were not our usual selves as we had quietened down somewhat. Tim's young lady was chattering ten to the dozen, whilst mine was still trying to get out the first sentence. Drastic action was needed here! The first bar loomed large and the party of fourteen joined two tables together, before Tee and Bob got in the drinks. Whilst ordering the drinks, two young ladies recognised Tee and Bob from the hotel and decided to join our group. They seemed delighted that the International Jet Set had got their comeuppance, as they had been ultra-snobby to other young ladies at the hotel. I suspected this was going to be an expensive night for Tee and Bob after losing the wager back at the hotel.

The growing party of sixteen then made their way to a big disco bar, very popular with the locals as well as the visiting Brits. Here, we bagged a huge corner table, ordered drinks and then sped on to the dance floor to show our prowess to the lovely ladies, who we had brought along. Some of the moves were so exaggerated and embarrassing! We thought we were really excelling ourselves and impressing our partners. Then the music stopped. The DJ announced that all young ladies must sit down as there was to be a competition for all the males in the room, with a prize of a Jeroboam of cava for the winner. We had to impersonate Mick Jagger and dance to "(I can't get no) Satisfaction". It must have been hilarious to watch a hundred males of all shapes and sizes strutting their stuff. The Judge was a model or Miss Lloret or something and she was very attractive. Tee in our group, who was probably the best looking of us all, made a bee line for this "model" and danced very sexily in front of her, unbuttoning his shirt slowly as he did so. After the music finished and the applause had died down, surprise, surprise!

"The winner of the bottle of cava goes to this gentleman near the front. Your name sir?"

"Tee."

"Congratulations to Tee and the rest of the dancers. There will be another contest, this time for the ladies, tomorrow night. Enjoy your champagne sir!"

Tee collected the bottle from the "model" and gave her a massive kiss with lots of saliva swapping and tongues etc. I suspect he had secretly arranged a meeting as well, but this could not be proven.

The bottle was absolutely huge, so the blokes were forced to drink the champers out of beer glasses, while the ladies were more refined and drank out of their cocktail glasses. This was obviously the place to be for tomorrow night around midnight, when the ladies could impress the blokes with their dancing.

Much more cavorting and drinking took place that evening/morning before we all headed back to our various places of slumber and other activities. Surely we must slow down after all this exercise.

Day 8

We were half way through our holiday. Where had the time gone? How much more could our bodies stand of this debauched way of life. Yes, we were young, but there had to come a time when enough was enough. Our kidneys and liver were working overtime, as well as other organs. Something had to give!

After our liaisons and activities, we were quite exhausted and spread out across two or three hotels in Lloret. Naturally, we had a get together at the Bella Vista after lunch, but it was oh so quiet. We had over indulged the night before on many things and the late nights were taking their toll. Around the pool were sixteen youngsters, flat out on sun beds. The waiters were extremely confused and were all standing by ready for the usual burst of sundowners. They flew into a panic when orange juice and tonic waters were ordered without a drop of alcohol in sight. The manager was contacted and he came round asking if we were alright. It was obvious that he had not had a death in the hotel and he didn't intend to start now. That evening as we disappeared to our various hotels for evening meals, a strange quietness and sobriety had descended on the group. It was as if our bodies were trying to tell us that they needed a break from constant debauchery. The manager of the Spar shop had phoned the manager of the hotel and apparently had asked if we had flown home, as we had been due another cava refurbishment that day.

So it was that after a few games of table footy in the bar and a few coffees, we wended our way to our pits for a decent night's sleep. Day 8 had been a bit of a washout. Would it last?

Day 9

We all woke remarkably early and made it down to breakfast for only the second time. The waiters were stunned! Platefuls of scrambled eggs and bacon etc. were readily and heartily scoffed. Even fruit was seen on the table, maybe due to the discussion the previous night about rickets and the plague.

We decided to take stock of the situation and because the stocks of Bacardi and cava were very low, we all went down to the Spar shop together. We were welcomed in by the manager like long lost friends, even though we had not given prior notice of our attendance. Naturally, we demolished the cava shelf and filled up the chariot with the goodies. We said adios to the manager as we made our escape up the hill to the hotel. After unloading the supplies in the cava bedroom, we made our way to the pool. Thunderous applause greeted our arrival, as it was still morning! Sun beds were commandeered and discussions were held about what to do for the rest of the day and evening. La Boda made it difficult to concentrate, as she was parading around the pool in the skimpiest of bikinis and flirting with everyone except us. Her thighs and breasts were beautifully tanned now and still in the right places. She really was a goddess. What had we done wrong? Pietro was despatched to find out what was going on, as he was the quietest and most sensible of the group. He talked to her for ages and then disappeared with her for a while.

When he reappeared, he announced that he would not be joining us for dinner and our after hours antics. Pietro had pulled La Boda! Had the world gone mad?

Well the afternoon was looming and lunch would be soon. We still hadn't decided on a plan of attack after the sundowner session. Someone came up with the brilliant idea of horse riding. Docker had seen a sign post pointing out of town to the hills surrounding Lloret, which said, "Equitacion". Tim translated this to mean horse riding. It sounded like great fun. Had anyone in the group been horse riding before? Only one! Me. I mentioned that my sister was a keen horsey person and that we once owned a horse. That was all that was needed to convince the boys that I had ridden in the Grand National at least three times. I had actually been on a horse about half a dozen times.

Lunch was quickly shovelled down and then we all went up to the cava bedroom for some much needed Dutch courage. The idea didn't seem so bad after a bottle of cava each and a very large Bacardi and coke. After the second and third Bacardi, we were all positively looking forward to it and so we set off down the road. Tee and Bob had joined us as well, so we had a full complement of troops.

We quickly staggered out of town heading for el rancho and came across a corral with some scruffy looking horses in it and an old ranch house. Juan sprang out to meet us and greeted us with warmth.

"*Buene tarde señors. Como estas?*"

Tim, who was good at Spanish, told Juan that we did not understand much Spanish, so that any instructions would be welcomed in English. He didn't mention the fact that we were half comatose with cava and Bacardi.

"Ah señors, that eez OK. I speak a leetle Ingles. I 'ope you 'ave a good time ere at El Rancho. We will be doing the 'orse riding across ze heels. As anyone ridden a 'orse before?"

Seven fingers were immediately pointed towards me and comments like 'expert', 'natural horse rider', 'has owned a stable with many horses' were being bandied about, too much for my liking.

"Zat ees good. I 'ave just ze 'orse for you."

Brilliant! After massive intoxication, that was just what I wanted to hear as Juan's helpers brought out this frisky looking dappled grey animal, already saddled and ready to go!

"Can you remember 'ow to climb on ze 'orse?"

"Yes!"

How difficult could it be after a skinful of alcohol? Surprisingly, after adjusting the stirrups, I climbed aboard and grabbed the reins tightly. The boys were well impressed! Lots of applause and "Ride 'em cowboy" came drifting my way. Juan then gave some instructions how to stop, start, go left, go right etc.

Next it was their turn. One or two faces went a little pale as some of them had never seen a horse let alone ridden one. One by one they were given a leg up into the saddle and duly made it, except for Simon who sprang into the saddle so vigorously, he flew over the other side and had to be given help to mount up by three of Juan's helpers.

At last we were ready to go. Juan was mounted on a beautiful looking bay and he gave us final instructions.

"Follow me, ze 'orses know wat to do. Zey 'ave done eet many times."

In fact it was OK. Off we went at a steady walk and the boys seemed to quite enjoy it. We headed out towards the hills over some dunes and it really was quite pleasant in the afternoon sunshine. There was just a nice breeze to keep the temperature reasonable. We were all in a line and I was near the back. Suddenly, my horse decided to bite the bum of the horse in front! This caused the horse to make a run for it and Juan had to bring it back and pop it back into line. Pietro who was on the horse at the time, squealed with 'delight' and was so excited by it all, he uttered a few swear words for good measure. The line of horses going through the dunes was quite orderly but mine seemed to have a mind of its own; it did not seem to respond to my tugging left or right on the rein. I could tell this wasn't a British horse, as those responded to my instructions. It was also quite a bully, as it kept nudging the horse in front which was being ridden by Docker. Docker had never been on a horse before and was very nervous. Gone were the witty comments and banter and in its place was a concentration we'd never seen before.

Just as we were all starting to feel relaxed, my horse took a fancy to Docker's horse and bit its bum hard. Docker's horse zoomed off in one direction and mine took off in the other. You could almost hear mine laughing, as we charged into the cacti and scrub. Fortunately, I managed to bring mine under control and we headed back to sanity, just in time to see Juan leading Docker and his horse to the front of the queue. All the boys were in fits of laughter and it wasn't until I caught up with them did I realise Docker had wet himself. Juan rode up to me and said, "You did good señor. You brought eem back."

He then proceeded to put a tether on my horse and gave it a hefty whack with his whip.

"Thees 'orse, 'e never learn!"

I was thus promoted to number two in the line and was being led by Juan. My horse wouldn't dare bite the bum of Juan's horse. It would have been in the knacker's yard before you could say "another cava?"

Somewhere in the hills, we came across a bar and Juan showed us how to tie up the horses to a rail. Mine was led away from the rest and tied up on its own at the back of this shack. Beers were ordered at quite reasonable prices. How did they get the beer here? How did they get the electricity here as there was no sign of a generator? There was nothing in view, apart from hills and dunes and cactus plants for miles. Very baffling! We got to know Juan a bit better and after five or six more beers, we were duly refreshed.

Off we went again, back to El Rancho. Strangely, this time we seemed a lot more confident. Juan had forgotten about the tether and I was in the middle of the line once again. From here, I sensed that the horses realised they were on their way home and they seemed to be moving a lot quicker or was it the effect of several beers?

Suddenly, in the middle of a very large sandy dune, my horse fell over to one side and I went flying into the scrub. My horse then proceeded to lie on its back and kick its legs into the air. I was totally unhurt by my fall. Again, it was probably due to the amount of beer we had consumed, making me totally relaxed as I was thrown off. Juan rode up quickly and used his whip a couple of times and brought the horse back to me.

"I am very sorry senor. Thees is a very nowty horse. 'E smell the water in the sand and 'e want to bathe. So sorry senor! Thees 'orse, 'e never learn."

Fortunately, this event didn't cause a stampede. The other horses were probably used to it. Why do I always seem to get 'the nutter'?

After we arrived back at El Rancho, we dismounted and there were quite a few sore bums and curious methods of walking. We said adios to Juan and his mates and headed back into town to relative sanity. Pietro duly disappeared and we headed into dinner after the customary refreshment with cava etc.

We had arranged to meet the girlies at a bar in town at ten o clock. We waited until half past and when there was no show, we were quite miffed and decided to have another night on the razzle. This inevitably led to mass drunkenness and eventually there was a falling out between two of our company, which led to fisticuffs. Everything was sorted by the end of the evening as we crashed out in our own beds at about 3am.

Day 10

Back to normal, the day started in the afternoon. A hearty lunch was eaten by all, before hitting the sun beds around the pool. After we had caught up on our sleep, we realised that we had hardly seen anything of the town and so it was decided to go and have a look at the town in the daylight. Hopefully, we would be back in time for 'sundowners'. Apart from booze, the only thing we had purchased was six spud guns. Maybe this was an opportunity to do some shopping and buy the occasional present for all our loved ones back in Blighty. Amazingly, Tee and Bob had turned up on their bikes, but were polite enough not to ride them into the pool as an aquarobics session had just started. They were left parked by our sun beds, which had the customary towels on them.

Once in town, it became obvious that some were better at shopping than others, so it was agreed that we should split up as and when required and meet back at the hotel for 'sundowners' at about 5pm. We could also show each other what we had bought for the folks back home. I had an inkling in the back of my mind as I had seen a sombrero with the biggest wingspan ever and the highest dome in the centre. Once I had finished acting daft with this on, I would give it to my mother to put plants in and she could hang it like a hanging basket. It would be the talk of the neighbourhood. After rummaging around in supermercados and back street shops, I at last found the very item. It seemed more expensive than I had thought, so I bartered with the natives and they knocked a few potatas off it. Before I returned for 'sundowners', I made one more stop.

It was after 5pm when I arrived back at the pool wearing my hat and as I turned the corner into the pool area, I was greeted with warm applause. Naturally, I played to the crowd and said in my best Mexican/Manchester nutter voice, "Hey Gringo! You wanna search my hat?"

Great hilarity followed as I carefully removed my hat to reveal a bottle of Bacardi, which had been balanced on my head. Yes, 'sundowners' was in full swing and the crowd of reprobates showed no signs of diminishing. This could be a good evening. Tee and Bob picked up their bikes to wobble back to their hotel and we agreed to meet at a bar in town later.

After dinner, we had a drop of cava before setting out on the evening's expedition. Tee and Bob were already in the bar when we arrived and what a surprise, they had a few girlies in tow, including the St. Helens' stutterer and her friend. The barman was delighted to see us all again as we downed a few cocktails. The St. Helens' stutterer must have already had a few, as she was quite lucid and her friend was still chattering to anyone who would listen. Pietro had not turned out; we suspected he had arranged another tête-à-tête with La Boda. That situation still confused us. Pietro was not a particularly good looking guy, being very thin and quietly spoken. He didn't say much at the best of times and his appetite for alcoholic beverages was not great. Perhaps that was what appealed to La Boda. Anyway, we were in full swing and the thought of Pietro and La Boda was quickly dispelled as we started to party the night away.

We made our way to the disco bar which we had come to consider as home. It was called the "Red Parrot" or "Pink Flamingo" or some other ornithological name. The huge neon light with the birdie symbol was a lighthouse for many a drunk, as it was so easily distinguishable from the myriad of other disco bars.

After a glass or two, we hit the dance floor with the girlies and were having a splendid time strutting our stuff. A couple of girlies looked very impressive too, with short shirts and tight tops. Indeed the St. Helens' stutterer was starting to look better and better as the evening wore on! Then, "Señores. Welcome to ze Pink Flamingo (or whatever it was called). Eet is now Señoritas night. Zat means all señors murst seet down. Tonight, ze señoritas will be dancing to ze fabulous Tina Turner and River Deep Mountain high! Ze best dancer will receive a very large bottle of ze finest champagne."

To massive applause and raucous singing, from the blokes mainly, the dancing kicked off. It was hilarious! Short skirts hitched up, high heels, coupled with alcohol, is a fine recipe. Those who attempted Tina's 'chicken walk' and managed to stay on their feet were definitely in with a chance of winning the large bottle. Our girlies, whether rehearsed or not, lined up and synched the moves. It was amazing! So much so that many of the other contestants stopped and applauded. At the end of the record, the applause and whistles for our girlies was fantastic. It was a foregone conclusion who had won. So the large bottle of Champagne was presented to all our girlies after much hugging and kissing. They brought the bottle back to our table and it was consumed with relish. From then on, the memory banks failed to register anything until the following morning/afternoon.

Day 11

As usual, day 11 dawned in the afternoon and there was slight stirrings and murmurings before I awoke to find a bra next to my head on my pillow, which was on the floor. As I slowly turned over and raised my head, which was pounding vigorously, I suddenly realised I had no idea where I was! I was on a mattress on a floor with three other people, one of the same sex and two of the opposite sex. On the mattressless bed were four other people, who I vaguely recognised. Everyone was in different stages of nakedness. Where was I? Who were all of these people? I couldn't quite focus. I didn't remember a damn thing! How did I get here? The last thing I remembered was drinking cava out of a beer glass at the Pink Flamingo. Well, I thought, I'm awake now. I'd better see what the damage was...

I gently opened a shutter to reveal the whole catastrophic scene. There were bodies and clothes everywhere. As things gradually came into focus, there were more stirrings and murmurings and I recognised everyone (minus clothes, which were scattered all over the room) from the previous night. Where we all were still remained a mystery.

One by one, people surfaced and made their way to the toilet to pee and to rehydrate. The nudity did not seem to bother anyone, who I suspect like me, were beyond caring. Someone bravely got in the shower and this started the ball rolling. There was not much conversation and there were only two towels, so we shared, one for the girls and one for the blokes. Trying to find clothes was ridiculous, as they were scattered all over the place. Most people finally got sorted, except Johnny couldn't find his under crackers. This didn't seem to bother him one iota. We eventually discovered we were in the girls' hotel room, how we got there, I have no idea. It was about 2pm and it was very bright outside. The boys then decided to make their way back to their hotel. So with lots of kisses and hugs, we said our farewells and thank you to the girlies, before trudging back to our accommodation.

When we arrived, two of our group were already there and wanted to know where we had been and what had happened. We knew where we had been, but as to what happened, we hadn't a clue! It must have been a great night/morning as there was very little sun bathing that afternoon and it was mainly concerned with drinking water and coffees. Between the four of us, we decided to take it easy tonight and just have a quiet evening in.

After dinner, we were still feeling the effects of the previous debauchery, although we were certainly a little perkier. Docker had the bright idea of a walk over to the girlies' hotel, partly to get some fresh air as it was cooler, but also a little female company would not go amiss. After all, the girls must be feeling as bad as us. This was agreed and so we set off.

Arriving at the 'Palace', we asked at reception where the girls might be. They obviously did not recognise us from the previous episode; we had made an effort and looked quite smart. We were directed into a very big lounge with sofas and armchairs and in one corner lurked the girlies, looking almost as bad as we were. We said hello quietly and moved in to snuggle up close and watch a bit of Spanish television on a fairly large screen. At regular intervals, we ordered coffees, water, lemonade etc and it was nice that they saw a different side to us. After two or three hours, the girls were starting to feel a little weary, so we took the hint and made our way back to the Bella Vista and unbelievably, were tucked up in our pits before midnight.

Day 12

We awoke at the crack of dawn well, 7.30am, which was about five hours earlier than usual. After dressing casually, we went down for breakfast for only the third time that holiday. Startled looks from the waiters again gave way to large grins and we troughed away quite merrily. Hardly having eaten properly for the last ten days or so, cereal, bacon and eggs etc. went down a treat. We actually felt good and there was a full complement for breakfast, even Pietro had turned up, but he refused to divulge where he'd been or what he'd been up to. He told us we would find out in due course. As breakfast progressed, it started to get darker and some very black clouds were rolling up. A few spots of rain appeared on the dining room windows, followed by a flash of lightening and a massive clap of thunder a few seconds later. This proved ominous. There was a break in the rain for about a minute and then it started to pour in buckets. The noise on the windows was deafening! As we had finished breakfast, we disappeared up to our rooms and this gave us a better view of the prevailing storm. The lightening was quite spectacular and the rain was torrential. As we peeped out, it was very noticeable that Tee and Bob's landing strip was a torrent of water and it was pouring down the side of the hotel. What were we going to do? After all, we were feeling very refreshed after our day and evening off the booze! Then…

Brilliant idea! All the lads grabbed a pack of cards and headed downstairs to the large lounge bar, where everyone was just milling about and generally doing nothing. Simon, who had the loudest voice yelled,

"Anyone fancy a card competition, whist or something similar?"

The take up was phenomenal! "If anyone has a pack of cards, please bring them down and we'll arrange the playing area."

With that, we began arranging tables and chairs in groups of four. If everyone came who had indicated, we would need about twenty tables. Everyone was seated and ready to go after about ten minutes.

"OK," said Simon. "The rules are simple. You need a partner and you should sit opposite your partner. You need to work together as a team. Cut for trumps and then it is simple whist. There will be thirteen tricks, so there will be a winning and a losing team. Further instructions will be given after the end of the first round!"

Off we went. The first round took about ten minutes.

"OK, now comes the tricky part. The winners stay where they are and the losers move clockwise to the next table. As soon as everyone is seated, deal the cards and away you go. When the game is over, exactly the same thing, winners stay put, losers move clockwise to the next table. There will be a drinks break after the next two rounds, if it is still raining."

Well, after the initial confusion about clockwise and anticlockwise, it all went according to plan, with much hilarity and introductions from table to table. People actually got to speak to each other and as a PR exercise, it worked a treat!

As the rain stopped and it started to brighten up, Simon decided to call a halt to the proceedings after a couple more rounds. How do we pick a winner to receive our last bottle of cava? Easy.

"How many people have stayed in the same seat?"
Silence.
"How many people have moved only once?"
Silence.
"How many people have moved only twice?"
One couple put up their hand and shouted "House". Thunderous applause.

"Ladies and gents, we have the winners. Please come forward and receive this expensive bottle of Champers."

More applause and one of the winners asked everyone to put their hands together for the organisers. More applause.

As it was lunch time, we cleared away the tables and chairs and went in for lunch. We all thought, "So this is how normal people behave!"

During lunch the sun came out and the pool area started to dry out rapidly. By the time we took our places on the sun beds, the first round of complimentary cocktails appeared from thankful guests. As the afternoon wore on, more cocktails and Bacardi and cokes appeared at regular intervals. Lots of folk appeared to tell us that it was a cracking idea having a card competition and thanked us for doing the organising.

By about 5pm, we were well oiled and having run out of cava, two of us were despatched to the Spar shop for additional supplies. As usual, we were greeted with smiles by the manager as we loaded up our chariot. However, he was a little disappointed with our half rations, until we explained in our fluent pigeon Spanish that we were going home soon. We shook hands and wended our way up the hill to the hotel with our final

Spar shop purchases. Of course the boys were delighted to see us as they hadn't had a drink in minutes and were looking distinctly thirsty. The sun was over the yard arm, so there was nothing for it but to broach a couple of bottles as we parked the chariot next to the sun beds with only 24 bottles of vino calapso.

'Sundowners' was a popular pastime with everyone around the pool and it was a great way to meet and get to know people. Quite a few holiday relationships grew out of the 'sundowners' culture, and it was good to know we had provided some entertainment for the inmates of Bella Vista.

After dinner, the usual fiasco of bars and discos commenced, with a small amount of alcohol in between. Funds were starting to run low, so we all were moderate in our intake. We tried putting our talents to other uses i.e. chatting up the ladies, but this seemed to cost even more. During a ladies loo break, the seven lads (still no sign of Pietro) decided to have a proper "lads night" the following night. The girlies didn't seem particularly interested in having a holiday relationship, so at about 2am we decided to go back to our pits, having had a very good day, despite the weather.

Day 13

The day dawned before midday and we dragged ourselves from our pits to shower and dress in swimwear. No-one seemed particularly interested in an 'early morning' cocktail. However, there was tremendous excitement as Pietro suddenly appeared at the pool. He was looking quite pale i.e. no sun tan and he looked shattered. I don't know whether he was ready for a Spanish Inquisition, but Johnny took on the role of Torquemada and gave him a right ear bashing! He had been kept in La Boda's room for days (hence the lack of sun tan) and apparently she not only had the body of a Greek goddess, but she was quite insatiable in the finer arts (hence Pietro looking knackered). We recounted some of the events that had befallen us and he seemed quite impressed. We told him that tonight was going to be a 'Lads Night', so he had better get himself prepared. We had heard that Tee and Bob were coming over as well later on, so it should be a full complement of troops out on the razzle.

Sunbathing by the pool was never an exciting prospect, as most of us had itchy feet and could not stay still for more than half an hour. So it was early afternoon when we broached the first few bottles of cava and immediately began to dispense liberal quantities of health and happiness around the pool, laughing, joking, silly walks etc. in the nice warm sun amongst friends. Could it get any better than this? Well, yes it could. Around about 4 pm when everyone was well oiled, two poncho clad figures with moustaches and sombreros came hurtling up the landing strip on roller skates and went straight in the pool. There was massive applause all round. Yes, Tee and Bob had arrived! The cocktails, cava and Bacardi went into overdrive. Tee and Bob removed their soggy ponchos, hats and skates and joined in the refreshments. They left on the droopy moustaches and they were sounding like the Manchester nutter with their fake Spanish accent.

After we had eaten dinner and drank a few aperitifs, digestifs and beers, Tee and Bob put their sombreros back on. As did I, Tim, Docker and Simon, who had bought some for brothers and sisters, back home. Johnny and Pietro were despatched down the road to purchase two cheap sombreros, along with fake moustaches for all of us. Off we went into town looking for fun and games. Gosh we did look good.

We were greeted in most bars with applause and some hilarity. The sight of eight amigos having a beer and lots of fun was a sight to behold. However, in one disco bar, after the usual hilarity, things turned a bit sour. One very drunk Englishman went up to Tim and told him he looked f***ing stupid. Now Tim is not known for his good temper and he pushed the drunk away. Then it all kicked off! A few insults turned to fisticuffs and glasses and bottles went flying. I was probably the furthest away from all the commotion, and turned just in time to see a glass coming out of the air towards me. Unfortunately, my reflexes were dulled by the vast amounts of alcohol and it smashed squarely on my forehead. The next thing I remembered was being in some kind of van, with blue lights flashing and a loud whoo whooing. No, it was not an ambulance, it was a 'Paddy Wagon' and it looked like we were en route to the local nick. Someone had put a large handkerchief or gauze on my forehead as I suspect I was bleeding, but was not quite sure. At the local nick, we were bundled out and thrust in a cell with a very bright light. I was lucky, as I was taken to a 'medical' room and patched up by a medic of some description, who kept tut tutting and mumbling in Spanish as he inflicted as much pain as possible to my forehead. After a while, I was deemed fit enough to join the others in a large pen/cell, where a discussion was underway about what happened. A massive bandage, the size of a hot air balloon covered my war wound. No-one seemed quite clear as to what had happened, so we settled down as best we could to wait for the consequences.

The consequences arrived early in the morning in the form of the biggest Spanish policeman you have ever seen.

"Eengleesh out!" was the formal greeting, not "Do you want jam or marmalade with your toast and coffee."

We staggered out and were given a stern lecture by another burly copper about the abuse of alcohol and what it can lead to. My head was hurting like hell and I have no recollection of what he said, even though he spoke very good English. After a while, we signed a paper again, I have no idea what it was and personally didn't care at this point. We were shown the door and had to find our way back to the hotel at about 7am. Thus began day 13.

We all disappeared into our rooms and crashed out for another few hours. It was difficult sleeping, as I had been bandaged by an amateur mummifier and had a huge wad of stuff on my forehead. We all managed a few hours! What had started as a happy and joyous evening with the boys had turned into a nightmare. Some of the boys went to the pool in the afternoon and apparently were very, very subdued. However, whilst recounting the tale to the assembled throng, they managed to see the funny side of it. I stayed in bed and finally made an appearance at dinner, complete with my two hundred metres of bandage. I knew it would happen. I was greeted with rapturous applause and shouts of "Ole!" but I was given preferential treatment by the waiters, so it wasn't all bad.

That evening, I decided to stay in and loaf about the hotel, watch television, chat to folks etc. A couple of the boys went out and I feared the worst, as Tim was going to look for the guy who had caused all the trouble in the first place.

I settled down to watch telly with Pietro. *Walkabout* was on and that was OK as it featured a few nudey shots of Jenny Agutter, and that was an added bonus. About halfway through the film, we had a surprise as La Boda and her friend decided to join us. La Boda immediately snuggled up to Pietro I did not feel like snuggling with yards of bandage around my bonce, but I made an effort.

By about 11pm I was back in bed after saying "Goodnight" to the girls and I suspected Pietro would not be seen again until the morning. Apparently, the others returned before 2am in a relatively quiet mood. I didn't hear a thing! So the penultimate day of our holiday ended in a quiet, controlled fashion, unlike much of the rest of it.

Day 14

We all were up for breakfast as we had the sole intention of topping up our tans, which were not brilliant considering we had been here almost a fortnight. I also removed my bandage, as it was starting to irritate me and I looked pretty stupid! We had a look round the cava room and found we had just under twenty bottles of cava left as well as a full bottle of Bacardi. All had to go today! It was going to be a dirty job, but someone has to do it.

After we had bagged the usual seats around the pool and set up shop, it was just about time for a wee drinky. We asked the management for a wheelbarrow, which they provided, and we bought some ice and filled it almost full. Then about half the cava was stuck in the ice and it was kept in the shade. A tray full of flutes was obtained from the bar and on the stroke of midday, we cracked a few bottles and filled the flutes. These were then handed round to all and sundry. Simon (the loud one) proposed a toast, "To the best holiday ever!" Everyone agreed and enjoyed the cava. More fabulous applause and very loud whoops as Pietro turned up, followed by La Boda in an absolutely stunning bikini, barely covering her ample essentials. She looked gorgeous, full of le joie de vivre, whilst Pietro looked knackered. He slumped onto his sun bed while she played to the crowd and went for a few lengths of the pool. How she was so tanned and Pietro was so white, remained a mystery.

Lunch consisted of crisps, nuts and other 'tapas', consumed with a large beer from the bar. The wheelbarrow was topped up with ice and cava and the cocktails and beer was flowing all afternoon as well. Our tans were looking a lot better by the time we adjourned for dinner. The wheelbarrow was full of water and there wasn't a full bottle in sight. Plans were being laid for the evening as we tarted ourselves up (and did some packing) for the final countdown.

After dinner, we had the small matter of twelve bottles of cava to attend to before we disappeared for the evening. We met up with Tee and Bob and all the girlies from their hotel, at the usual bar. There were some extras from our hotel too, who had wished to join us for the evening entertainment and who had very kindly helped us to dispose of the cava, making about twenty in the party in all. The usual cocktails were ordered and we had a giant kitty as it would have been too complicated to order separate drinks for everyone. Pietro was to look after the kitty as he was the most sensible amongst us and we made him promise not to disappear with La Boda!

After a few drinks, we made our way to the 'Flamingo', our favourite disco bar, just as Loop di Love was booming out from the speakers. This was one of those terrible Euro-crappy songs that the Spanish are so good at. We immediately all hit the dance floor as some people were just too shy and within minutes, the dance floor was a writhing mass of humanity. Gone were the inhibitions as the alcohol started to kick in, arms were waving, legs were flexing and most people were screaming the banal lyrics at full blast. It was fantastic that everybody danced with everybody else, even La Boda spread her charms around and towards the end of the evening we even managed a slow number with her, and made sure we were in very close contact, which she liked very much.

The night/morning continued in this vein and we did not want it to end. But unfortunately at around 3pm it did. We had drunk and danced the night/morning away and it was time to wend our way back to the hotel. As we hit the fresh air, quite a few of us became more than a little wobbly, and so it was decided that everybody would make their way to our hotel to crash out. Being on the 7th floor and well away from civilisation, we were unlikely to be disturbed. There were about five rooms and about twenty of us so beds were split, mattresses were added to the floor with the odd sheet and we all stripped off and piled in. There was very little hanky panky as most of us were too full of antifreeze to be capable of anything. There were just lots of cuddles and within about thirty seconds, we were all asleep.

Day 15 – homeward bound

AAAAAaaaah!!!!! What was that noise? It was a bloody alarm clock and it was 8am. Gawd! Then reality dawned. We were due to be picked up from the hotel to get to the airport at 9am. Lots of bleary eyed folk were roused and despite the swearing, were made to get up. By the time everyone was awake and revving, we had fifty minutes to ablute, pack and get downstairs with our suitcases. It was even worse for others, as they weren't even in the right hotel. Tee and Bob and the pride of girlies staggered downstairs to leg it back to their hotel. Fortunately, they were last to get picked up by the coach and we said we would delay it as much as possible to give them extra time.

We managed to get our acts together and got to the ground floor with our suitcases in time for a snatched croissant thing and lots of fruit juice. We said our goodbyes to the Manuels (waiters) and scraped up enough potatas to give them a decent tip for putting up with us, just as the coach pulled in to the front. We staggered out, handing cases to the driver and then making excuses that we had to go to the toilet, which gave Tee and Bob and his crew an extra 10 minutes!

Finally we were off. Although slightly queasy and very tired, we managed to get Tee and Bob on board and we all zoomed off to the airport. The bus was silent as we were asleep within seconds.

At the airport, check in and any security was a blur. We were all wearing our fine sombreros and wearing our false moustaches. Gosh, we did look good. Passing through duty free, we spent the last of our potatas on the requisite booze, regardless of the allowance, and finally headed across the tarmac to the waiting plane. After carefully removing our sombreros and stashing them in the lockers with our duty free stuff, we settled down for a two hour snooze.

We were rudely awoken by the plane wheels hitting the tarmac and screaming to a virtual crawl. It was then we realised that we had exceeded our duty free allowance and would have to pay duty on the booze. Not a chance we thought! How can we avoid this?

As we moved through passport control, we all put on our sombreros to collect our baggage from the carousel, and then quickly moved through the 'nothing to declare' channel at the customs station, where we followed the Manchester nutter's example and gave everyone a fine rendition of...

"Aye yi yi yi! Charlton is better than Pele" and lots of Lah lahs as we didn't know the words. The officials quickly intervened and moved us on. There were lots of ...

"Ey gringo! You wanna search my hat?"

But the custom officials were immune to all of this banter and quickly moved us along, as we were starting to cause a backlog.

Just as well really, as each of us who had big sombreros managed to stash a litre bottle of Bacardi under the centre. That was a job well done.

We found our hired cars and disappeared into the sunset.

2-The Lake District

As teenagers, we were always keen to show how grown up and independent we were. Most of us had a part-time job of some description, whether it was delivering newspapers, magazines etc. or doing some kind of manual labour. It was generally hard work and had to fit in with our studies, but it did provide for the little luxuries we enjoyed – beer, women and song. It felt good to be able to afford things some of our friends could not and helped us to value money. Just to show how grown up we were, we all decided to plan and finance a holiday together. This was to be a massive decision and we started planning a cycling holiday to the Lake District in the summer holidays. Some of us had been two or three times before, hiking on the fells and up the mountains, but a cycling holiday was something special as the Lakes were extremely hilly.

Nine of us got together and poured over maps whilst drinking home brew. We tried to keep the route as level as possible but inevitably, there were going to be steep inclines on some days. Money was collected to pay the fees at youth hostels and this was sent off as postal orders to the various establishments en route. After about a week, we got confirmation from the wardens of the hostels and we were then booked in. Once confirmation had been received, there was no turning back or all the money would be lost. This was the easy bit! Seven of us already had bikes in various states of repair, and the design of some of them left a lot to be desired. Two of our group did not have bikes at all! Why they chose to come on a cycling holiday if they didn't have a bike is beyond comprehension. However, they had about three months to get sorted and we had the same to get our bikes in some kind of shape, complete with 'panniers' to carry our clothing.

As the weeks wore on, everyone was gradually getting their stuff organised, except one lad Grenville. Grenville was notorious for 'cocking things up' and so he earned the nickname 'Dizzy'. He kept telling us that his neighbour had offered to lend him his racing bike and he would assemble it for Dizzy as the moving parts were kept in oil to keep them clean and lubricated. He had managed to borrow a set of panniers too, which went over the back wheel on a frame. Everything was looking good and we decided to get our bikes together and go for a long ride to get in some training. We assembled at Barnes' house, complete with panniers or in my case, two 'haversacks' strapped to the frame. Everyone arrived on time except Dizzy. Pedalling the five hundred yards to Barnes' house had become an ordeal, as the chain had fallen off twice and one of the tyres was slowly deflating. He was spotted walking his bike along the road heading for Barnes' house. We quickly fixed the chain and some of the more competent cyclists, whipped off the wheel and tyre, found the puncture and mended it. Was this an omen?

Off we set all nine of us in single file, along a pre-planned route which was not too busy. After about 15 minutes, it was obvious that one of us was missing, but the lads in the front did not realise this and pedalled on. For the few of us who stopped, it was decided that we had to have a method of stopping the front runners if there was a problem. We decided there and then that everyone should have a whistle and give two blasts if someone needed to stop. But, who was missing from our group? Yes it was Dizzy. After about fifteen minutes, he turned up pushing his bike. The chain had come off again and he had no idea how to put it back on. We set to and put the chain back on and set off after the others, who were waiting for us about a mile ahead. They all laughed as we told them why we had stopped.

We decided to let the slowest in the group lead the way (Dizzy), despite the fact he hadn't a clue where we were going. But we kept him right and despite the chain coming off his bike another six times, we managed the fifty mile circuit alright. Everything looked OK for the big start the following weekend.

As the following Saturday approached, we all managed to check our bikes and make sure they were in the best possible condition. All except Dizzy, who really hadn't a clue about the mechanics of the bicycle and trusted totally what his neighbour had said, "It's an excellent racer in superb condition." If he had been truthful and said it was a racer in need of a lot of care and attention, then at least we would have been prepared for the worst. Instead, Dizzy was blissfully unaware of the real state of his cycle.

We all set off after our parents had given us last instructions and cautions. All looked good for the first half mile and then the inevitable! We had not even got out of town before we heard blasts on the whistle and as we looked back, we saw Dizzy by the side of the road with the chain in his hand. Now it doesn't take a degree in mechanical engineering to get a chain back on a bike, but to Dizzy it might have been easier solving a complex mathematical equation while juggling sticks of dynamite. However, we quickly got it sorted and set off again. This time we managed about five miles before the chain came off again. It was obvious that there was something dreadfully wrong with the linkage. As we had about ninety miles to cover over some hills, this was going to be a long day.

As the chain fixing was slowing us down rapidly and was happening every five or ten miles, we decided to put Dizzy in front. The road was relatively straightforward and because of his slower pace, we gave him a head start of about five minutes. The peloton then set off and we were amazed that after five minutes cycling, Dizzy was still nowhere in sight and a large hill loomed. As we got to the top of the hill and decided to have a short rest, we heard a feeble cry coming from the hedge bottom, "Help! I can't move."

As we strained our eyes, there was Dizzy in a ditch with his bike on top of him! He couldn't move as the bike was wedged in by the sides of the ditch. We could not believe it and roared with laughter before dragging the bike off the unfortunate cyclist. His left pedal had come off and this had caused him to hit the bank and virtually somersault into the ditch with the bike on top of him. Fortunately, there was no water in the ditch and apart from a bruised ego, there was little damage to the person.

The bearings on the pedal were completely cream crackered, but we managed to cobble it together somehow and fix his chain as well. We decided that as soon as we reached civilisation, we would strip the bike and see what new parts were required. Everything seemed to be broken on this 'super bike'.

Eventually we reached our destination, the youth hostel in Penrith, after calling in to various shops looking for cycle spares. We didn't find any, but we did find a shop selling 'powerballs', so we bought one each. For the uninitiated, a powerball is exactly what it says, a small ball about the size of a billiard ball, made out of compressed rubber. When released with the minimum of force, they will bounce off virtually any surface at random angles and keep on bouncing for a long time. When released with more than the minimum force, they zoom all over place at great speed and cause havoc in a confined space like a closed room! Just what we needed! We finally landed at the youth hostel after travelling for about ten hours. It seemed as if the majority of this time was spent putting Dizzy's bike back together!

We were given a dormitory in the attic space at this lovely youth hostel and quickly made our beds and got our belongings organised. By the time we had had a shower, the gong was rung for food and we legged it down the stairs for food as we were all starvin' Marvin.

After dinner, we were assigned to do the washing up and as there were nine of us, we rattled through it. Even though we were very tired, we still had the strength to walk the mile into town and search out a really sad pub where we managed to get served, even though we were under age. After a couple of beers, we all started talking gibberish; it was really having an effect after all the exercise we had had. The slow walk back up the hill was really exhausting and we collapsed thankfully into our pits and slept soundly.

The following morning we bounded down for breakfast and after the cereal and cooked food, we ate as much toast as we could stuff into ourselves to give us extra energy. We were only going to Keswick, which was just along the road, but first we had been told of a fantastic bike shop in Penrith and we decided to call in there and see if we could fix up Dizzy's bike. After we had packed our kit, someone thought it would be a good idea to release our powerballs in the attic space, as it was full of alcoves and sloping ceilings. This we did with great effect and the thud of nine powerballs hammering off the walls and ceiling about twenty times did not go down too well with the youth hostel warden, who immediately kicked us out and told us not to come back. Off we pedalled into town to find the aforementioned bike shop.

We arrived at the shop and dismantled the bike in the yard at the back. It was a mess! The chain was the wrong size, both the wheels had been attached without any oil/grease to the bearings, the pedal that broke had seized solid and was useless, and the front forks were twisted, so much for the "excellent racer in superb condition." We negotiated a price to fix all of this and with their help, we were soon on our way to Keswick.

It was so much easier not having to stop every few miles and fix chains etc. and we arrived in Keswick in time for lunch. The bikes were locked up at the youth hostel, which overlooked the River Eden (which flooded dramatically 2015/16), and we had a wander round town. We found a tea bar in the less touristy area and scoffed beans on toast or similar. Two of our group then decided to release their powerballs in the toilet area of the café and as they smashed around the walls to the delight of the two idiots, the proprietor arrived and duly asked us to leave as we were frightening the other customers. As we were the only ones in the place, this was hard to believe. However, confrontation is not what we were about and so we duly left.

Back at the youth hostel, we checked in and were allocated a dormitory for twelve. As no-one else arrived, we were able to spread out and used the remaining bunks as sofas. We were fortunate to have had quite a relaxing day and were first in to the showers before dinner and got dressed into the usual teenage uniform of jeans and T shirt.

After dinner, we headed out to sample the delights the wonderful town of Keswick had to offer. Naturally, it was centred around the local pubs, where we sampled a few of the local ales. One of the beers in particular proved very popular. Jennings was a local brew from Cockermouth, just up the road, and it went down a treat with thirsty cyclists. So much so, that some of us staggered back to the youth hostel ready for the curfew and lights out.

The following morning arrived in the nick of time. It was pouring with rain and so we celebrated this after breakfast by releasing nine powerballs in our dormitory. Yes, it had the same effect as the last place and we were ejected from the youth hostel into the pouring rain. As we donned our bright yellow cycle capes, we set off for our next hostel at Grasmere. We had intended to park our bikes and climb Helvellyn, but the summit was shrouded in cloud and it was still pouring down. It was not easy cycling, as the rain seemed to be driving in every direction and it was difficult braking, so we had to take extra care. Fortunately, the traffic wasn't too heavy and we made frequent stops to make sure Dizzy was still with us. The repairs seemed to have done the trick as we never stopped once because of breakdowns.

The following day it was brilliant sunshine again and we started to make our way to the west of this beautiful county, eventually staying at the Eskdale hostel. We arrived there just in time before another torrential downpour. We knew that night there would be no pubbing, as the following day we were to navigate the treacherous Hardknott Pass followed by Wrynose Pass on our way to Langdale. We amused ourselves by playing silly board games and chess, which were freely available in the youth hostel, before having an early night.

The following morning after the best breakfast so far, we set off for Hardknott. On the map it didn't look too bad but when we arrived, we were flabbergasted. The incline was horrendous and we had to push our bikes an awfully long way. This was energy sapping as our panniers were full of stuff and very heavy. The roads were still wet, but thankfully it was not raining. At the top, we had a well-earned breather and the view was magnificent, looking over to Wastewater (the deepest lake) and Scafell Pike. The way down was incredibly steep and with the wet roads, it took a lot of concentration and effort to apply the brakes. There was a great danger of skidding and worse still, brake failure. However, we managed very well until the last mile when we released our brakes and 'went for it.'

All was going brilliantly until a car pulled out of a lay-by without any indication and drove off like a maniac. The guys at the front missed the car by inches, brakes were slammed on, there was lots of skidding and three bikes ended up in a heap in the middle of the road. Even though we were not wearing helmets or any protection, the majority of us remained almost unscathed apart from Big Al, who had skidded sideways along the ground and his knee was ripped open and bleeding. A number of people in cars jumped out when they saw what had happened, and fortunately one of them was a nurse who had a large medical kit in her car. She immediately went into action and patched up Big Al. She also offered to take him to the nearest hospital, as Big Al's knee was a complete mess. She was a wonderful lady and after we dismantled Al's bike and put it into the boot of her car, she drove him to the nearest hospital. After he was patched up, she took him to the nearest train station and put him on a train home, together with his bike in the guard's van. Truly a Good Samaritan and a large bunch of flowers was sent to her on our return. Big Al was out of action for about six weeks, but he was still alive and still had his powerball.

The rest of us made our way tentatively up and over Wrynose Pass to Langdales, and eight very shaky cyclists booked in to the youth hostel. That evening, we toasted Big Al's health in the local pub and had a few more just to make sure the toast worked properly. The following morning we emerged from our pits slightly the worse for wear, but ready for the day ahead. We missed Big Al, not only because of his sparkling wit and repartee, but also because he was a very experienced cyclist and he knew the area well.

After checking out of the youth hostel, we jumped on our bikes and set off for Ambleside. The weather was fine and the roads were dry, such a difference from yesterday. Ambleside was reached in double quick time and we parked our bikes at the youth hostel before having a stroll round the town. Two or three of our group needed the toilet and we found a brilliant one near the town centre. Now how brilliant can a public toilet be? Well this one was so fantastic that we all piled in. It was tiled from top to bottom apart from the roof, which was wood. After we had done the business, powerballs were readied and released as one. It was fantastic, there were eight powerballs whizzing around the public convenience and thudding against the ceiling. It caused uproar and pandemonium inside and a few of the users quickly zipped up their flies and vacated the premises at speed. We were on our own and the powerballs were released again with even more venom and more thudding from the ceiling. Raucous laughter ensued as some of the balls struck members of the group. The laughter was not to last as a member of the local constabulary stuck his head round the door and narrowly missed being decapitated. This brought our antics to a sudden end as we were booted out of the convenience.

After dinner that evening we found a hostelry and proceeded to sample the local produce. One of our group had smartened himself up and was looking really dapper. Consequently, he had the third degree from the rest of us

"Are you not coming to the pub with the rest of us?"

"Er no. I'm just going to have a walk round town."

"Why are you all dolled up?"

"Well, just in case I meet someone nice and we have a nice time."

"Have you planned something already?"

"Course not!"

With that, he had gone walkabout. Now Westy was not a particularly good looking guy, but we thought he was trying to score with the local populace. We were very dubious, but if there was not a lot happening, we would visit a few other pubs and see if we could spot him.

After the first few beers, we started chatting to some ladies from Leeds, who were very good company and were probably as randy as we were. They were good value and funnily enough there were seven of them too, so it was a good match. We decided to move on to another pub to sample a different atmosphere and lo and behold, there was Westy with the most amazing looking young lady. She had long dark hair, a tight top and a very short skirt harbouring the most delicious legs. Wow! We all thought. How has Westy managed that? Naturally when he saw us, he went as red as a beetroot. However, we thought we would cut him some slack as we were being well entertained by our current company.

As the night wore on, we were starting to 'pair off', and one or two of the young ladies were getting frisky which was nice! They were staying in a rented house just up the road, so it would be very chivalrous if we escorted them home. There was one problem however, the youth hostel door was locked at 10.30pm and it was after 10pm now. We were on the ground floor in the annexe, so it could be possible for one person to let the rest in through the window. We drew lots (names in a hat) to see who would have to go back and it turned out to be Dizzy. Off he went after saying 'night night' to a disappointed girlie, and off we went into the realms of the unknown. Westy had gone too.

We disappeared up the hill towards a rather nice 4/5 bedroomed house with a driveway and front garden. The lights were dimmed, music was put on and the groping and saliva swapping began. Everyone seemed to be having a nice time and one or two disappeared from the main action. It seemed an ideal combination but unfortunately we could not stay in Ambleside, as the hostels had been booked and paid for in advance. At about 2am, we gathered in the huge lounge, said our goodbyes and disappeared down the hill towards the youth hostel. We crept round to the annexe and tapped gently on the window. No answer. We knocked harder. Still no answer. Finally we hammered on the window and Dizzy appeared half asleep. We piled in through the window just as the lights came on in the main building. The window was shut and we were motionless for about a minute. Finally the lights went off and we clambered into our pits for about five hours sleep. Westy was not back!

The morning dawned as mornings often do as a teenager – too early. Westy had not returned! What were we to do? We couldn't leave without him. Perhaps he had met the love of his life and was on his way to Gretna.

We needn't have worried. In he strolled, whistling, just in time for breakfast.

"Well?"

"Well what?"

"What happened? How did you get on?"

"Same as usual, right leg over first."

That was the end of that conversation.

To celebrate our conquests, we decided to let loose the powerballs in the annexe. This was not a good idea, as two windows were broken and we were charged a large sum by the warden to fix them. When we had paid up, he threw us out. We deserved it

All too soon, our holiday was coming to an end and apart from being thrown out of three youth hostels, two pubs, a café and a public convenience, it was a roaring success and we enjoyed it thoroughly with the exception of Big Al, who had a hole in his knee for his trouble.

3-Skiing Tonale 2004

During my years as a teacher, I had the honour of organising or participating in about twenty ski trips for kids from whichever school I was teaching at, at the time. They were always great fun and it was a pleasure, in many cases, to introduce a healthy activity to youngsters. Of course some had been skiing before with friends and relatives but for many, the thrill of going down the piste unaided on wooden planks for the first time, was truly awesome. In all of the twenty or so trips that I attended, there was only one person who disliked it. Going with the younger age group was fantastic and had its advantages, as usually they were so tired at the end of the day that they went straight to bed without any shenanigans. This enabled the staff to indulge in a few sneaky beers in the hotel bar, knowing that the children were tucked up in their pits!

This is an extract from a diary of one of those trips. Four members of Staff and two former gap year students were awarded the CDM after their arrival back in Leicester at the end of this trip. Mr Jones, Mr Garnett, Mrs Summers, Mrs Wilson, Rob Curtis and James Duckham received their honours at a special ceremony behind the Science block on that Saturday evening. Plasters, bandages and valium were also the order of the day!

The trip started at Stansted, where a number of Year 8 pupils terrorised the airport security with their impersonation of F1, driving on baggage trolleys around the check-in desks. This was quickly followed by the World 'Goodie' eating championships! Whatever the distraction, it seemed to work, as we had hardly had time for more than 4 Big Macs before we were ushered aboard the waiting Dakota and strapped and gagged firmly in our seats to await departure.

Our flight was coated with mediocrity, as we were allowed to breathe occasionally and we soon reached our destination of Bergamo. Passport control proved no opposition to our F1 drivers and with the Italians screaming and waving their arms frantically, we were bundled aboard the waiting furniture wagon.

After a short nap, we arrived at our resort, Tonale, a charming resort in the Alps. However, our hotel was not full of Alpine charm; it was more of a blot on the landscape! Visions of Nelson Mandela Towers in Peckham sprang to mind, but not quite as luxurious. The evening meal was followed by the customary lunacy called a ski fit and after a brief sojourn around the block, we settled into our pits for a good nights' sleep.

Daylight dawned at the 'Towers'. Food was excellent and soon we were off to the pistes. After haggling with an Italian bandit at the ski shop for the privilege of keeping our boots dry, we were on the slopes in glorious sunshine.

The skiing was marvellous (is that the first time I've said that?) and the piste was relatively uncrowded. Lunch was held at a really good Alpine restaurant, where the inmates scared all the old ladies by hurling thousands of snowballs from a great height. This was hailed a great success and so they decided to do this whenever there was a crowd of people gathered.

Our ski instructors were extremely patient and also very good; they came complete with flak jackets and riot shields. Word of the Leicester Mafia had spread fear and trepidation through the resort! After skiing each morning with an instructor, the various groups were whisked away by the staff for an afternoon of terpsichorean delight in glorious sunshine. This was the order of the week.

Lots of entertainment was provided including a visit to a local bar to watch some European qualifying footie. Yes, England was playing an important match and therefore we were obliged to watch the Italians! This seemed quite reasonable to the Italians, but did not go down too well with the Leicester Mafia. However, it was good to see the Italians lose, so the evening was not a complete disaster.

Many adventures followed, both on and off piste. One of the highlights was when someone spotted our ski rep! Another of the highlights was leading the beginners down a very steep black run on the last afternoon. They all made it slowly but safely and were overjoyed at the achievement. Some of the more advanced skiers attempted a free fall route down the same mountain and they too arrived at the hotel safely. Naturally, as custom would have it, a flag was rescued from a local restaurant.

After a last night full of excitement and silly sketches, we were strapped into our hammocks ready for the journey home. We said '*Arrivederci*' to Nelson Mandela Towers the following morning and soon we were winging our way back to Blighty.

We arrived back at Leicester full of plumptiousness and joie de vivre. Marvellous!

Chapter 5

Taxing Days

The tax office

Have you ever wondered why your tax affairs sometimes seem chaotic when dealing with Her Majesty's finest?

After leaving college, it was quite difficult to obtain a teaching post. Many of the local authorities accepted people en masse on the assumption that there would be a number of resignations in the authority, and therefore they would fill the positions with the 'pool' applicants.

The year I left college, I too was accepted into the pool of prospective teachers and I eagerly awaited the name of my new school. However, three days before my wedding, I received a letter from the Authority advising me that "resignations from teachers had not reached the expected level and so there is no longer a position for you in the county."

Aw bugger! What a great wedding present. I had been doing various temporary jobs after leaving college and it looked like this might have to continue into married life, delivering meat and pies in a mini-van was not going to get me fame and fortune. Neither was working in the hardware department of a massive builders' merchants. Therefore, a cunning plan had to be the order of the day. As this was not forthcoming, I applied for and got a position in the Inland Revenue as an Assistant Collector of Taxes. Never having been in an office before, I really had no idea what to expect.

On my first day, I was introduced to the staff in the large, modern office of a ten storey tower block in the centre of a busy town. Apart from one other bloke, I was the only man in an office of about thirty-five. There was a varied collection of ladies. Many of them were quite young, but there were some very smart, more mature ladies. Smart dress was essential for both male and female inmates, as we sometimes had to deal with the general public face to face. The boss of the office was a fierce looking spinster, who ruled with a rod of iron. Milly never let standards slip in any area and was frequently heard giving a good ear bashing to the ladies who had lost concentration on work for about an hour or so, whilst discussing knitting patterns etc.

Fortunately, I was assigned to a desk opposite the other bloke who was called Andrew, and we seemed to hit it off straight away. Whilst the ladies were discussing knitting and cooking etc. during the day, Andrew and I would be talking about sex, football, sex, cars, sex, drinking beer and sex. It was the year of the short skirt and some of the younger fraternity flirted with Andrew and I, knowing full well that we were married, and they caused many a palpitation by flashing huge lengths of thigh and beyond. In fact, I am sure that sitting provocatively on mine and Andrew's desks, flashing various items of underwear, became a better pastime than knitting patterns and menus. If Milly spotted any of this alluring behaviour, she leapt out of her office and gave the offending hussies a mouthful, whilst apologising to us and doing a bit of spinster flirting herself! I can't deny we didn't enjoy it. Being the centre of attention and encouraged by some very fetching wenches was not unpleasant – in fact, to some extent, we encouraged it. Nowadays, they would have been hauled up for sexist behaviour or provocative something or other. Back then, we all had a sense of humour and we were grown up enough to cope with such behaviour. The 'do gooders' hadn't quite made their stand at that time. Andrew and I had to come up with a number of ways to 'get our own back' for the titillating and suggestive behaviour.

Two of the typists were very pretty and had extremely long legs and very curvy figures. They were not against wearing low, see-through blouses and very, very short skirts. They were probably the worst/best at winding us up and were often strolling through the office, flashing their wares at the boys. We would often get an internal phone call from them inviting us into their glass office as they "couldn't quite understand" the Dictaphone letter. This meant we were exposed to large expanses of thigh and buswams and although we never did anything to make physical contact with the girls, it was just as well the 'thought police' were not around!

Part of our job was to communicate with the general public either by phone or by letter, with the typists receiving a Dictaphone copy of the letters to be sent. It was all done on electric typewriters and earphones, as computers had just been invented and were not in offices yet. Andrew and I would submit these letters for typing and after the customary summons to the glass office for thigh and booby viewing, the letters were then given to Milly for proof reading before despatch. Occasionally, after some particularly hectic thigh and buswam ogling, we would intersperse the odd letter with absolute gobbledygook, and the typists would type all of this as they were on autopilot and did not actually read the letters. So a typical letter would look something like:-

Address etc.

Dear Sir,

With reference to your query regarding your Schedule D outstanding payment, I am delighted to tell you that this has now been removed. In respect of the stress caused by this undue demand, we are pleased to inform you that your account has been credited with £500.

Yours faithfully etc. etc.

Sometimes the typists would spot this codswallop before it got to Milly, whereas on other occasions, it reached Milly's office and she almost blew a fuse! If this happened, there would be little thigh and buswam ogling for a couple of days until she simmered down.

One of our other tricks was to tape down the black connectors that the telephone receivers rested on. Consequently, when we had done this, usually in the lunch break, we would phone the person internally and when they lifted the receiver, the phone continued to ring! They would be really perplexed and started to shout "Hello" ever so loudly. Then we would put our phone down and the ringing would stop. After replacing their phone and mumbling, we would ring again with the same result. After the third or fourth time, the mumblings got really loud and things like this

"Well, it was working alright this morning", were quite common. This was a particularly merry jape to inflict on new colleagues, and was even better if we could get into the cashiers' office. We didn't dare do it on Milly's phone.

Very often we would have a delivery of stationery or other office equipment, and this was delivered by two or three different drivers. One of the drivers was a hoot, as he was always playing tricks on the ladies who signed the receipt for delivery.

My first encounter with this chap was on a day when I was assigned to deal with the counter and the general public. If someone came to the counter, they rang a buzzer and I had to rush into the counter office area with the speed of a thousand gazelles. If it was a query I could not deal with, I had to fetch the appropriate person concerned. Enter driver 1.

Buzzer sounded and I bounded into the counter area, where I saw a chap dressed in smart blue work overalls. He introduced himself and showed me his ID, telling me he had a delivery for the typists. I said I would fetch the typist concerned and she could sign for it, as well as inspecting the brown paper parcel on the counter. After the customary thigh and buswam flashing, the typist made her way to the counter. We then heard very little as the parcel was no doubt being inspected and the various appropriate documents signed. Suddenly, there was an ear piercing scream and the aforementioned typist burst through the door of the counter area into the main office. She continued to scream and sob for a minute or two, as

Milly (who had exploded from her glass palace), tried to ascertain what had happened.

Andrew and I disappeared next door to see the delivery man laughing like a drain. Eventually he calmed down enough to tell us that the typist had inspected the parcel and everything was fine, so he asked her to look at the paperwork which was in an envelope. As she opened the envelope, it 'whirred' and moved just as a large insect would do, and she screamed and ran. Apparently, he had slipped into the envelope, a metal hair grip which had a button wound on an elastic band and stretched between the ends of the hair grip. On release, this thing had 'fired' and made a sound on the paper as well as jumping around. Very effective we thought and started to laugh as well. This was short-lived as Milly came into the counter room with a face like thunder. After she saw that it was three blokes, her mood changed and instead of the massive haranguing the delivery man was due, a mild telling off was forthcoming. She did like the blokes, did Milly!

On his second visit, the delivery man kneeled down behind the counter pretending to be a dwarf, and asked for the other typist to sign. She had never seen him before and so she was bursting with the news that a dwarf had delivered her stationery.

On another occasion, he somehow attached an indoor firecracker to the parcel that went off as the parcel was unwrapped. By this time, however, it caused very little furore as everyone was getting used to his antics. He mentioned that he would have to think up something special for his next visit as we were getting wise to his tricks. Well he certainly did that – or so I thought.

The large town where I worked was roughly divided in half by the river and there was heavy industry on either side of the river, employing tens of thousands. There were thirty-one ladies who looked after the tax and revenue on the north side of the river, and Andrew and I looked after the tax and revenue on the south side. How this imbalance came about, I don't know. However, we did manage quite well. Part of my brief was to collect the PAYE from the heavy industry on the south side, and I frequently had to call them to remind them that this massive sum was due. If it was not paid on time, huge interest was charged on a daily basis, so it was necessary to get the payment in or there would be severe consequences. Normally, a cheque for tens of thousands of pounds (if not hundreds of thousands) was sent or delivered to the cashiers, who then passed it onto us after logging it.

One week during a hot summer spell, the phone call went out to remind them that payment was due. On the other end of the phone was a panicking assistant who told me that the paymaster/treasurer had been knocked down on his way to work and was in intensive care in the local hospital, and therefore could not sign the cheque. I suggested that as there were three signatories who could do this, there should be no problem. He replied that the M.D. was in the Bahamas and the other chap to sign was in the Far East on a business trip. There did not appear to be a solution, so I asked if the assistant could sign the cheque. He informed me that he had to have two other signatures as he was just an assistant and all he was allowed to do was draw cash. This seemed a bizarre situation, so I reminded him that the deadline was fast approaching and he had to get something sorted out.

A few days later the buzzer went in the counter office and as I was on call, I went through to the inner sanctum. In front of me was a chap wearing smart blue overalls with a large brown paper package done up with string. As we were expecting a stationery delivery from the practical joker, I didn't think it was anything out of the ordinary, although I did question the fact that our usual man was not here.

"Hello. Where's our usual man?"

"Pardon!"

"You know, the bloke who always does stupid things!"

"Sorry. I don't know what you mean."

"You know, the mad bloke who sets off firecrackers and stuff."

"I'm sorry. I have no idea what you're talking about. I've just been sent to deliver this parcel and get a receipt."

The bloke started winking at me. At this point I thought something very strange was going on and then I twigged! Old matey boy had sent his 'oppo' to deliver the parcel, to totally confuse us.

"Thank you," I said, and casually picked up the parcel and threw it out of the open window. I didn't expect what happened next.

The blue overalls man ran out of the office yelling and screaming at the top of his voice, and ran into the cashier's office, whereupon all the lifts were shut off and the metal grilles at our entrance came down. Alarms were being sounded and panic ensued. What was going on? Had I just thrown some stationery out of the window? Well no

The Chief informed me that I had just thrown tens of thousands of pounds from the heavy industrial company out of the window, as the only way they could pay their PAYE was to do a bank draft for cash.

Ooo-er!

He went on to mention that I had to go down the stairs after the alarms and grille had been turned off, get a step ladder from the caretaker, climb onto the ground floor flat roof and pray the parcel was still intact. With my tail very securely between my legs, this I did. As I slowly climbed the step ladder, thunderous applause rang out as every window of the ten storeys was jammed with people watching my progress. Thankfully, the parcel was still intact and all the cash was retrieved safely.

I nearly lost my job over that incident.

After the 'cash out of window' debacle, I kept my head down for a few weeks and kept the thigh and buswam ogling to a minimum. I was still getting grief from all in the office except Milly, who took me to one side in her glass palace and told me to put it all behind me, as apparently I had great potential and a flair for figures. The last part was certainly true as I glanced out of the palace to where the ladies were discussing the latest colours and styles of tights, by revealing more than just thighs! Milly was being really mumsy and very comforting at a stressful time. But wait! Had Milly applied some extra rouge and lipstick? It seems having two blokes in the office had set new parameters in the 'make-up stakes' and it looked like 'everyone' was trying to appear more appealing. Milly also said that as I had mastered the office basics, she had a very important job for me to do. What could she mean? I was soon to find out. All bad debts and underpayments of any description were sent directly to Milly if the time limit for payment had expired. She then decided on the next course of action, usually in the form of a visit from one of the cashiers. This on the whole had limited success as it was very difficult to obtain the dosh or the necessary evidence for a prosecution in the County Court or Small Claims Court.

Enter *Inland Revenue 007*. Me.

I was given half a day's training and then I was to be sent out on the road to collect the tax owed from these debtors. I was given a list of debtors, the necessary ID on a posh lanyard type thing and written authority to obtain payment there and then, either cash or cheque. My mission was to start the following Monday and I was asked if I had a suit to wear. Naturally, I had my wedding and funeral suit, but I had to borrow a stunning tie from a friend. The Monday loomed large and I arrived at the office on Monday in my best bib and tucker, with highly polished shoes, and was given the usual treatment for looking super smart – wolf whistles and wiggly bottoms in tight skirts from the girls. Even Andrew couldn't resist and he started a chorus of "Diamonds are forever" and everyone joined in. Even Milly was smiling. As most of the debtors lived and worked very locally, I was to walk as much as possible to the various addresses, but if I had to take a bus, I was to keep the receipts. I was amazed too that I even got a lunch allowance. I finally had a look at the list of 'baddies' and apart from the usual scrap yards, taxi firms, private bus companies, Chinese restaurants and takeaways, I was stunned at how many solicitors were on the list. Apparently, they were the worst at paying death duties and tax for their clients. They much preferred to hold on to money and keep it in their accounts, earning considerable sums in bank interest.

I arranged my route, which Andrew thought was far too optimistic for my first visit. However, I set off to my first call which was Anderson's Scrap Metal. Mr Anderson had not paid any PAYE tax for three years, despite it being noted that about ten different people were seen working there. Andrew said if I got past the Alsatians, I will have done well. Mr Anderson must have been telepathic or have some kind of Inland Revenue radar, as he was at the gates to welcome me. I approached this large fellow who was dressed in quite smart jeans and a T shirt, with trepidation. As I had nothing to lose, I decided to get my retaliation in first. "Good morning. Mr Anderson I presume. How nice of you to welcome me to your humble abode. I presume you know who I am and why I'm here?"

"Mornin'. Yes, I know where you're from, but I've told those useless buggers time and time again, they've got it all wrong. I don't have any full time employees, so I don't owe them any tax."

"Well, Mr Anderson. I have certain evidence that you do have employees and that you pay cash in hand for their services. Now, how you run your business is no concern of mine, I just do what I'm told and collect the money. Could we discuss this over a cup of tea and maybe there is scope for some kind of compromise?"

"Whaddya mean like?"

"I've been given some authority to dismiss the underpayment or at least part of it if I see fit."

His eyes lit up on the words "dismiss the underpayment" and he invited me into his office and put the kettle on.

"You are the first one of them bastards that's ever got further than the main gate. Now, tell me what you mean by dismissing the underpayment."

"OK Mr Anderson, cards on the table. Just let me finish and then say what you think. According to our records and calculations, you owe £3329. If you can furnish me with payment for £2500, I can write off the rest. What do you think?"

"Mmmm. If you can make it £2000, we might have a deal. Are ya sure you can do this? I would need it in writing."

"I am sure I can do this and I will give you the arrangement in writing, and you will have written confirmation from my boss within a week. £2000 it is then. Do we have a deal?"

"That sounds OK by me. Just wait there, I won't be a minute."

With that he gave me a cup of tea and disappeared into the inner office. He was there for a while and returned with large bundles of notes and he counted out £2000. I had never seen so much money and bearing in mind this was the early seventies, it was quite a considerable sum. We shook hands and he handed over the money. I then wrote out a disclaimer for any excess amount on headed note paper and pocketed the money.

"Do ya wanna a drop of the hard stuff in ya tea?"

"Oh no, thank you. I've got some more negotiating to do after this."

After the tea, he escorted me to the main gate and we shook hands again.

"First time I've ever shaken hands with the Tax Man" was his parting comment. I was well chuffed with the outcome, but I had no authority to do what I had just done. I just hoped Milly and Co would be as pleased. After all, this tax avoidance had been going on for years and no-one had got anything out of Mr Anderson, so I hoped the £2000 would make them see me in a good light. With my inside pocket bulging with notes, I made my way to the next challenge.

Round 2: Mr Tao's Chinese restaurant, the Chin Foo. This restaurant had a takeaway attached to it and was very popular at lunch times and also during the evening. Every time anyone goes in, they are served by a different waiter/waitress. There must have been dozens of employees yet strangely, Mr Tao had paid no PAYE tax or any other tax for that matter. He drove around town in a very big car and was instantly recognisable as he was the largest Chinese person (in every direction) that I had ever seen. As I entered his takeaway emporium, he was behind the counter talking to a young man, so I joined the end of the queue. As I approached the counter, I flashed my ID card and was met with the response:-

"Solly. No speak Ingrish."

"Oh yes you do!" I countered. "I've just heard you chatting with the customers."

At which point Mr Tao went bright red and seemed totally lost for words. I thought I would help him out a little, so I offered, "We need to have a little chat in private if that's OK."

He then ushered me through a side door into a room next to the kitchens, where I spotted about six people working at the stoves. The smell was absolutely sublime!

"I will talk. My daughter will listen too. She keeps records of business," Mr Tao went on to say.

After a few minutes, a beautiful young girl appeared carrying a large book and a notepad. She was dressed immaculately and was stunning in her totally westernised dress. In a local accent bearing no hint of Chinese she said,

"I keep all the records, which are handed to our accountants at the end of the financial year. My father has little to do with this side of the business, so everything should be directed towards me."

I reintroduced myself and produced my ID and my letter of authorisation, which she studied for a minute or two. She asked me what I wanted as the business was not too profitable and all the staff were part-time and therefore paid no PAYE. I began my spiel.

"Well according to our records, you owe about £7000 in various unpaid taxes. This is an estimate as we have had few or no returns from you or your accountant. I have a letter showing the estimated charges for a business this size, and I have noted the Jaguar and the large house on the edge of town."

She studied the details and then spoke to her father in Chinese. After he replied, she stated that the amount was grossly inflated and the business owned the Jaguar which was used as a delivery car. The large house on the edge of town was bought with a loan from relatives and a mortgage. There was no way they were able to pay this amount. She also mentioned the continual hassle the family had from the Inland Revenue and maybe we should arrange to see the family solicitor. I then said,

"Perhaps we could come to some arrangement."

"What kind of arrangement?"

If you gave me a cheque for £4000 now, there would be no more hassle from the Inland Revenue and the rest of the debt would be written off."

She then relayed this to her old man in Chinese. He replied and she got quite annoyed with him and started shouting. It was all getting quite tense. He stood up and dwarfed us both, yelling and waving his arms as he did so. She then did the same. It was getting like an Italian comedy. More arm waving and shouting followed, then silence as she sat down and he walked out.

"I'm very sorry about our family discussion, but Pops is very old school and has never paid tax before. If there was any trouble, he just gave a donation to another family group and the demands seemed to disappear."

Along with the people concerned, I thought, Gawd, what have I got myself into?

Mr Tao returned a few seconds later and thrust a cheque on the table and walked out. Mademoiselle Tao explained, "My father says thank you. I told him he would not get a better offer than yours. I thank you too. If you could now write a disclaimer for the rest of the estimated tax, that would be good. I assume we will get an official document stating this in the very near future?"

I assured her she would and for some stupid reason, I put my hands together and bowed whilst I thanked her. What a plonker! Funnily enough, she did the same.

I walked out of the restaurant thinking I could be in a lot of bother here or I could turn out to be the hero who had got money from a scrap merchant and a cheque from a Chinese Restaurant. So on to my next port of call.

Round 3: Payne and Feers Solicitors. You would expect that solicitors were the most lawful and helpful people. Well they are, except when it comes to tax, death duties etc. A number of people had been despatched to these solicitors and a promise of money/cheque was never fulfilled. So I was on my way to try and extract some dosh for the death duties of one of their clients. This was a complicated case that had been dragging on for a couple of years, with numerous claims, counterclaims and legal garbage from relatives of a wealthy resident and former mayor of the town. Again, I entered the premises with trepidation after devouring a large sandwich for lunch. It was early afternoon and the receptionist indicated that the solicitor dealing with the case was on his lunch break. He had been gone for about an hour and was not expected back for another hour. I said I would wait. It was before the days of mobile phones and games etc. so I had to amuse myself in the cavernous waiting room by reading something called a newspaper. Naturally, after page 3, I moved rapidly on to the back pages and read the sports section. After a while, I engaged the delightful young receptionist in conversation. I wondered if she knew any of the ladies in our office, as she frequently crossed and uncrossed her legs revealing acres of tights and thighs. I thought initially it was rude to ogle, but I realised she was doing it for my benefit, so it would have been bad mannered of me not to watch the movements intently.

All too soon, the solicitor came back and I distinctly smelled alcohol on his breath after his two hour lunch break. He was a jolly, portly man with a large moustache and the usual pinstriped suit. After the usual introductions, he asked about the health of our Chief and wondered why he hadn't appeared in person. I simply told him he had been before and it was now time for the 'heavy brigade' to intervene. His jovial mood changed and he became more serious, explaining the 'whys and wherefores' of the case, which went totally over my head. He was rabbiting on and on and I think I had a 'cobblers' moment as I interrupted his boring monologue.

"Look Mr Payne. I am not really interested in all of this. All I need is some large payment from you as an interim measure until the legalities of the case is sorted out. I understand that the estate is worth a few million and therefore the duties are considerable. I am not leaving this office until I receive some kind of payment on account. It will keep my Chief happy, me happy and I'm sure you will be happy to enjoy your long lunches without the intrusion of the Revenue!"

He appeared quite stunned and he never said a word as he sat back on his black leather chair. After a few seconds, he reached into his drawer and pulled out a chequebook on which he wrote out a cheque for £10,000. I duly accepted this, wrote out an official receipt, said "Good afternoon" and buggered off. As far as I knew, he was still stunned in his shiny black leather chair as I made my way back to the office. It was just after 3pm when I arrived back and was ushered into Milly's glass palace.

"Please sit down," said Milly. "Now tell me how difficult it was to extract money from those three musketeers. I don't expect much as it was your first assignment."

"I have a confession first," I said. "I did get some money, but for the first two clients I told them their debt was to be written off."

"Good grief," said Milly. You didn't have the authority to do that!" I could tell she was not amused.

"Yes, but I did get some money!"

"You definitely should not have done that. Only I and the Chief have authority to do that." She was still not amused!

"Yes, but I did get some money!"

"I don't know what the Chief will say. I'm going to ask him in to hear this."

Yes, but I did get some money!"

"Just wait and I'll get him."

"But Miss Reid, (I was being really formal now), I did get some money!"

With that she disappeared. I felt like a naughty schoolboy in front of the head teacher. Even the office ladies looked dubious and I caught sight of the typists actually pulling their skirts down to reveal LESS thigh!

Milly arrived back shortly with the Chief in tow. Milly asked me to explain the situation to the Chief, which I duly did, getting redder in the face. He put his head down and rubbed his chin thoughtfully. In a slight Irish brogue he asked,

"Did you get any money?"

"For the umpteenth time, yes, I did get some money!"

"How much did you manage to get?" said the Chief.

As I emptied my pocket and laid the cash and two cheques on the table, there was a gasp from the two in authority.

"There's £2000 cash from Anderson, a £4000 cheque from Mr Tao and a £10,000 cheque on account from Payne and Feers."

A very long silence.

Then a grin appeared on both their faces, followed by a slap on the back from the Chief.

"Well done son!" said the Chief.

I had gone from villain to hero in about thirty seconds.

As the summer progressed, I suddenly got an offer of a teaching job in Liverpool and because I had spent three years drinking in the College bar, I decided to accept this or else my training would be wasted. Reluctantly, I handed in my months' notice and the look on Milly's face was devastating. I think I was Milly's protégé and she had often told me I had a natural flair for many aspects of the job, particularly screwing money out of bad debtors. No-one was irreplaceable, so it was no surprise when Jason turned up after two weeks. He was to be my replacement and Andrew and I were to train him up and show him the ropes. As it was my last two weeks in the office, I hoped it was going to be fun. It was. Jason was six feet nineteen tall and had black hair and an olive complexion. He was clean shaven, which was not the norm in those days. All in all he was a good looking bloke and he was single, which was a like a red rag to a bull for the ladies in the office, who were not against a little flirting. After the initial introductions and the drooling by the ladies, he was assigned a space at my desk as it was quite large. There was still ample room to play wheelies on the castor chairs and Andrew and I began to 'show him the ropes'.

Firstly, we told him about Milly and her little foibles. We stressed the fact that it was wise not to upset Milly, even though we could get away with minor misdemeanours as we were blokes. Despite being a spinster, she had a wicked glint in her eye at times and she was not against a little flirting (in a spinster type way) with the boys. We mentioned that Milly ruled the ladies with a rod of iron and sometimes reduced them to tears if they were naughty. That brought us nicely on to the second item regarding the thigh and buswam ogling. Right on cue, along came the two typists with 'dictaphone queries' for Andrew and myself. Poor Jason nearly fell off his chair as he looked across the desk at typist 1 bending over Andrew and revealing a delightful see-through bra. He hardly had time to collect his thoughts, when typist 2 sat on the corner of our desk and revealed the colour of her underwear. I told him quietly to close his mouth and proceeded to go over this fictitious query, whilst giving most of my attention to the vast expanse of flesh that was thrust my way.

After the typists had disappeared, we advised Jason to give as much attention to busty substance and thigh as possible, as it was the standard in the office. Also keep one eye on the glass palace in case Milly thought the ogling was lasting too long. He mentioned that he thought he would enjoy it in the office. Hardly surprising really, considering the amount of 'material' on display.

He took many of our silly initiations in good spirit, particularly the sellotape over the phone receiver connectors. We kept this up for nearly a day before he twigged what was happening. Then when he tried to stand up, Andrew had tied his shoe laces together. The 1000 paperclips strung together around his chair kept him amused too. The 'piece de resistance' was when we inserted a page 3 nude into a report that he was asked to do for Milly.

At first she seemed quite annoyed, but saw the funny side of it and obviously knew that Jason had been set up by us.

Yes! I thought Jason would fit in quite nicely.

Chapter 6
Work Days

The wonderful world of teaching

Kid comes home from first day at school. Mum asks, 'What did you learn today?'

Kid replies, 'Not enough. I have to go back tomorrow.'

Most people remember their first day at school for different reasons. I remember vaguely my first day as a pupil but more importantly, I remember my first day of teaching – vividly.

My first teaching appointment was in a typical sixties inner city boys school. It was a mass of concrete and glass and had one block of three floors, whilst the rest of the school was two storeys. It was surrounded by the usual metal railings, with a bar of about twenty cms. along the spiky top. There was a small car park for staff and visitors at the front and large double gates (also with a spike on the top), which was the only entrance and exit. It was situated on the edge of Toxteth in Liverpool surrounded by a myriad of terraced houses and it was a really run down area. I think at the time it was classed as a social priority area. Many of the houses still had outside toilets down the yard, and there was a fair amount of 'gang' activity in the neighbourhood.

I rolled up in my car on the first morning and parked it at the front of the school, hoping I hadn't taken anyone's parking spot. I got out and looked for the main entrance/reception or even a door that looked welcoming. There wasn't one. I noticed a very big man in the centre of the playground and he was smoking a cigarette. He was about six feet six inches tall and weighed about eighteen stone. He looked like a rugby player. I strolled up to him, carefully avoiding the boys playing footy with a tennis ball and before I could say anything he said, "You must be Jack. I'm Rod and we're on playground duty all of today. That means morning, break and lunchtimes. Our job is simply to make sure the kids don't kill each other before lessons start."

After that introduction, he grabbed a little kid and told him to go and get two coffees from the staff room for the teachers on duty. I couldn't see anyone not following instructions given by Rod as he looked so big and fearsome. We chatted and he told me a few ins and outs of the school, where the smokers went, about discipline etc. Apparently, discipline was very strict; it was the only way to keep order in such a rough area. Fear was the key and the headmaster had that in bucketfuls. I had yet to meet this charming chap.

When the coffees arrived after a few minutes, Rod casually took out a packet of cigarettes, handed me one and lit them up. I questioned this and he told me that it was quite OK.

The kids were running about in the playground and there were a few minor scuffles, but as soon as Rod approached, they were all over. I was still having difficulty tuning in to the scouse dialect. Lots of new words for me to learn, most of them derogatory, but I was starting to get the hang of it. The coffee was nice and Rod seemed an amiable chap. He said I would be introduced to the staff tomorrow morning just before assembly. I did not have a registration group or a form to look after as I was a new teacher, and new teachers were excused this particular duty in their first year, unless there weren't enough 'experienced' teachers left.

About five minutes before the bell, Rod called over a black kid and when I looked, his pristine white shirt had blood splattered all down the front.

"What happened to you son?" says Rod.

In the broadest scouse accent, which I had trouble following, he answered,

"Aer it's awright Ser. Three white honkies thumped me on the way to skule. Don't worry Ser, they're divs. I'll get 'em back."

After a little while exchanging banter, the bell rang and they all lined up as if by magic, in the playground. At this point, Rod told me to grab a cup of coffee at break time and head straight for the centre of the playground. The little kids like to feel protected from bullies who try to greed their tuck shop snacks off them.

The morning went very well. I was introduced to my Head of Department, Uncle John, who was Head of Science. He gave me my timetable and showed me the stock room where coffee was made, fags and pipes were smoked and lunches were often eaten. Fortunately, I did not have any classes until after break, so I became ensconced in one of the labs and had a good look round, preparing myself for the deluge after break. I watched Uncle John teach a fifth form (Year 11) physics lesson and I was very impressed. John looked like Albert Einstein – grey/white hair sticking out all over, but with rimless specs perched on his nose. I was to later find out that he was an amazing bloke.

The bell for break finally went and I managed to grab a cup of coffee before the stampeding hordes of the rest of the staff appeared. I met Rod in the playground and we did our duty, then the bell, now off to lessons to teach general science to a first year (Year 7). It wasn't too bad, once we had finally got over the language barrier, it was relatively plain sailing. I yelled at one kid as John had told me to do, stamping my authority and discipline on the class. Word would soon get round that I would stand no nonsense!

Very soon the bell for lunch sounded and Rod and I went straight to the front, as we were on duty. This was shovelled down at speed and before you could sing a verse of "The Mersey Tunnel's three miles long and the roof is made of glass", we were out in the playground for an after lunch fag and a cup of coffee. There were lots of kids milling about and coats were put down for the customary goals. Teams were picked and the lunchtime footy session was underway. Plumes of blue smoke could be seen emanating from behind the sports hall at various intervals, and everything seemed hunky dory. However, as if by magic, the little kids stopped playing footy and everyone stopped what they were doing. There was a huge great space in the middle of the playground, as everyone moved quickly to the side. Only Rod and myself were left in the middle. As we looked up, three young white guys came hurtling through the school gates, followed a few yards behind by the black kid with blood on his shirt and a cauliflower nose. This time, he was wielding a machete and running after the white kids. The three in the front were running flat out towards us when they looked up and saw us. The three split and went in different directions. This seemed to confuse the machete carrying maniac and he paused before legging it after one of the lads. They were heading straight for the spiky railings and the black guy was closing in. It seemed like I was watching some kind of movie! As the boy in front approached the railings, he sprang towards them and grabbed hold of the spikes. At the same time, he managed to get his foot on the bar near the top and was starting to haul himself up, when...Whoosh! the machete came down and split the boy's jacket so it hung like curtains. He managed to fling himself over and run off, with his jacket still hanging off him.

Rod said to me, "Come on mate. Let's ****off out of here before we get hurt," just as three police cars raced into the playground. We held our ground and the police quickly disarmed the youth and bundled him into a car. Apparently, the boy who was machetied was unhurt but in shock, as the machete just cut through his blazer and a bit of his shirt. Well that was exciting! Not bad for the first day of my teaching career. Could it get any worse? Oh yes! As a probationer teacher, I was expected to observe the odd lesson or two from the more experienced staff. John was very relaxed about this and said I could please myself how much I observed. His philosophy was simple; the only way to learn how to teach was to adapt your own style and get in the classroom and do the business. Watching John go through his stuff was truly epic! He was a natural teacher and he was well practised in the art of controlling kids as well as actually getting them to learn some basics. My first observation was a typical 'John Lesson' He had a small group of fifth year (Year 11) remedials (as they were called then) and was attempting to teach them about pulley systems and how to lift things more easily with a system of pulleys. One nauseating skinhead youth kept interrupting and making 'witty' comments.

"Or ay ser, what's the point of all this', I'm never gonna use it."

"The point is Jefferson that some jobs require you to lift large weights and you have to know how to do it safely."

"Burime neva gonna wherrk, so itsa load o' cobblers."

"Some idiot might take you on as an apprentice car mechanic. You would then have to know how to lift an engine out. Also, if you're on a building site and you want to lift a heavy weight to the first floor, you could make it easier by using a pulley system."

"Burime neva gonna wherrk, so itsa waste o' time."

"If you don't want to listen, then just go and knock on the headmaster's door and tell him that."

"Er it's alright ser. I'm happy here."

It sounded like the youth was better off in the lesson than visiting the headmaster. I later discovered why.

John continued with the lesson and the kids were getting the hang of velocity ratios and mechanical advantages, despite continued interruptions by Jefferson. He had a large pulley system suspended from a beam on the ceiling. The beam was about six metres off the ground and very substantial. After about the tenth interruption by Jefferson and the tenth 'put down' by John, John finally had had enough.

"I need a volunteer. You'll do Jefferson. You will need some support. Grab hold of his arms and legs boys."

Which, they duly did, despite protests and a mouthful of abuse from Jefferson. He was not a big lad but he knew better than to argue with some of the gorillas in the class. John produced a few lengths of rope and tied his arms and legs. Jefferson was then stood vertically and more rope tied his arms by his side. So he was mummified in rope and hooked on to the pulley system. By this time the abuse had reached a crescendo, but John and the other boys seemed totally unfazed by it all. After a brief discussion about velocity ratio and mechanical advantage, Jefferson was hauled up towards the ceiling and let out a series of screams punctuated with foul abuse.

"Well as you have all worked well, apart from one, I think we should go and have an early lunch," Much agreement followed and so the end of the pulley system was tied securely round the leg of a bench and Jefferson was left trussed up, hanging about a metre from the ceiling, whilst everyone went for an early lunch. The abuse continued until the lab door was finally closed.

After lunch, John and some of the boys went back to the lab to see if the abuse had abated. It had. Jefferson was then lowered back to terra firma and untied. Not a lot was said, but Jefferson had learned his lesson and was never any trouble again in Physics. There was no explanation from John as to why he did this, but apparently he did stuff like this on a regular basis, and his lessons were a 'sea of calm' compared to the mayhem which was taking place in the rest of the school.

Some of my lessons were OK and some were just chaos. It seemed to be that the new teacher or probationary teacher got most of the lower sets. It was good in one sense, because it helped you develop a style in order to survive, and also some of the stuff you taught might actually enable these boys to pass the odd exam. The classes were very mixed when it came to ethnic origin. Liverpool is a true cosmopolitan city and there were boys whose parentage was from India, Pakistan, Ireland, Greece, Italy, the West Indies, Turkey, China, Hong Kong and Indonesia. It seemed very unusual at the time to see and hear some of these nationalities with a scouse accent. There was very little in the way of race related incidents, the machete incident being an exception. I learned quickly how to deal with certain 'incidents' in the classroom. It was not unusual, for example, for a boy to lash out at another boy whilst in class. It was generally accepted as the norm. Teachers, however, could not be seen to condone this behaviour and so we had to learn a strategy to cope with this. On this front, I had an excellent teacher in John, who taught me most of what I put into practise, forgetting most of the text book stuff I learned at college.

One boy was the bane of my life (and everyone else's). Punishments did not seem to work with him and even John had trouble at times with him. He did not seem to have many friends, as he was so awful. He was so bad during one lesson, that I had no alternative but to send a boy for the Senior Teacher.

A few minutes later, the door burst open and a voice bellowed,

"YOU BOY. HERE."

It was the headmaster. The Senior Teacher was occupied with another incident and the Headmaster had heard the continual knocking on the senior's door. The Headmaster was a former Brigadier in the Army and he walked around school with his swagger stick tucked firmly under his armpit. He was a giant of a man and had a voice to match. His swagger stick had a brass fitting at both ends and they were very highly polished.

On his command, the 'naughty boy' came forward, head bowed and stood in front of the giant. Whereupon, the Headmaster started to beat the boy with his swagger stick and ranted and raved at the same time. The poor boy covered his head and cowered in a heap whilst the blows rained down.

"YOU (whack) WILL NOT (whack) CAUSE TROUBLE (whack) IN (whack) LESSONS (whack) EVER AGAIN (whack). DO YOU (whack) UNDERSTAND? (Whack)

Of course, by this time, the boy was a gibbering idiot and sobbed uncontrollably, which was a sign of weakness and resignation.

At the end of the beating, he stopped, calmly tucked his swagger stick into his armpit and casually asked me,

"Is there anything else I can do for you?"

"No thank you Headmaster," I replied. I was in shock as were the rest of the boys.

Needless to say, I never sent another boy to the Headmaster or Senior Teacher.

Uncle John was revered by all the boys and I could not understand why, apart from the fact he was a brilliant teacher, was always calm, rarely had a bad word to say about anyone and he genuinely liked kids. One of the teachers took me aside one day and explained about Uncle John; not only was he Head of Science, but he looked after the local youth club three or four evenings a week. The local youth club consisted of two old and knackered prefabricated buildings dumped on a demolition site next to the school. They had linked them together and put wire netting over the windows to prevent breakages. The boys had cobbled together some cash and got a second hand table tennis table and bats. There was power into one corner of the room (apart from the lights) and when the heater was not plugged in, John had provided a kettle and scrounged some old mugs so that the boys could have a cuppa. He presided over the goings on and the boys were delighted to have somewhere to go in an evening and meet their mates. It kept them off the streets and out of crime. The boys loved this place and took great care of it. Any threat to the sanctity of the place was dealt with appropriately.

John was always trying to scrounge stuff from the council and local shops, businesses etc. Times were hard, but he managed a few items of furniture and someone actually provided a coffee bar. John often wrote begging letters for stuff and one such letter was sent to Fred Davis, asking if he knew of any cheap second hand snooker tables. As expected, there was no reply.

One day, whilst teaching Physics to the dimwits, there was a knock on the John's lab door and a man in blue overalls appeared.

"Err, are you McGrory?"

"Yes."

"Gorra delivery for you. It says, deliver next to skule. What's tha' all about."

"Best have a look then. Can you wait five minutes for the bell?"

"Yeah. I'll be outside in me van."

When John got outside, there was a big blue truck which matched the colour of the bloke's overalls and another car/van with another four blokes in it.

"What's going on? I haven't ordered anything!"

"Says on this ticket to deliver to McGrory at a site next to the skule. You're McGrory and the only thing next to the skule is that battered prefab. Signed F Davis. Does that mean anything?"

The light was starting to dawn on John as the truck doors were opened and there was a nearly new snooker table, cues, rests, balls, scoreboard, chalk and any other accessory. John was flabbergasted. Not only had Fred Davis provided an almost new table and accessories, but he had shipped it and sent four technicians to erect it.

The snooker table became the pride and joy of the boys and they looked after it with immense dedication for many a year.

Teaching reminds me of the quote from 'A Tale of Two Cities' by Dickens "It was the best of times, it was the worst of times, it was the age of wisdom, it was the age of foolishness."

There were good times and there were some very sad times. During my first term, I was on playground duty with another member of staff, when a young lad came into the playground with only socks on, no shoes! The other member of staff called the lad over and the conversation went like this, "Hey, Johnno, where's your trainers?"

"Or ay ser, it's me brothers turn to 'ave 'em this week."

"OK son, pop over to the sports hall at break and I'll see if there's an old pair over there for you."

"Nah. It's alright ser. It'll be my turn for them next week."

"Well Johnno, pop over anyway. These trainers have been in lost property for ages. They're just gonna get chucked out at the end of term, so you might as well have them."

"OK ser. I'll see."

I asked the question, after he had gone, "What was all that about?"

Rod told me that he came from a family of six boys and his mother scraped a living to clothe and feed the family. Father was a docker, earning good money, who spent everything down the pub and rarely had enough left to provide for his family. If the kids weren't in bed before he came in from the pub, they all got a good belting and if it wasn't the kids, it would be his mother.

As we went back to the staff room, Rod organised a whip round from the staff and collected enough money to go down to the local department store at the end of the road, in his free lesson, and buy Johnno a new pair of trainers. However, when he got them, he went round the back of the sports hall and dirtied them and caked them with mud. He did this because firstly, Johnno would not accept charity and secondly, if he had gone home with a brand new pair of trainers, his dad would have thought he had stolen them and he would have got a belting!

I later found out that Johnno had reluctantly accepted the trainers, only because his socks were wearing thin.

The police were always in contact with the school, as the chances were that if there was any petty crime in the neighbourhood, our boys were responsible or at the very least, knew who was. Usually, their first point of contact was Uncle John. He had probably taught many of the coppers and knew more about them than the Force did. They bypassed the Head, as they knew what a bully he was.

One particular morning, I entered John's stock cupboard and found him in conversation with a massive policeman. After the usual introductions, I gleaned that one of the boys was getting arrested and taken into custody every single night for breaking in to the local department store. He was a sixteen-year-old youth who had special needs and therefore the police were reluctant to press charges, as a custodial sentence or any other sentence was meaningless. John advised the officer that he would look into it and let him know what the score was.

That lunchtime, he asked to see Jake, the aforesaid youth and questioned him about his nightly activities. It appeared that Jake used to break in through a back window of the store and just wander around the store. He never did any damage or made any kind of mess, he just enjoyed the darkness and the solitude. Of course he eventually set off the alarms and the police arrived to see the youth just ambling around the aisles. After locking up the store and taking Jake down the local nick, he was eventually let go with a strong warning. Needless to say, he had forgotten everything by the following day and the episode was repeated that night.

However, I could see John was having a word with him and he was drawing something on a bit of paper; maybe it was a reminder to keep out of trouble or another plan. After a few days, John got a phone call from the local copper who was singing John's praises. Whatever John had said to Jake had worked a treat, and he was no longer being arrested every night.

I asked John what he had said to Jake to put him on the straight and narrow. He replied without a flicker of emotion in his voice, "I showed Jake how to bypass the alarm system."

What could I say?

School sports were always challenging in Liverpool, as there was great rivalry between Liverpudlians and Evertonians. This 'friendly' banter between the two clans, turned into full scale war on match days. Quite often blood was spilled, and the local hospitals prepared for a big influx of clients on 'Derby Day'. The P.E. staff at school tried their best to channel this aggression in a controlled manner, but inevitably things often got out of hand.

Liverpool is a city not known for its prowess in cricket, so it was quite a brave decision by the school or P.E. department to enter the Liverpool Schools knockout cricket competition. I hadn't even seen a cricket bat, let alone seen a game being played! However, in the first round of the competition, we had been drawn away to Carmel School, a posh Jewish School, and the match was in less than two weeks' time. Once the draw was known, all the summer footy matches in the playground turned to cricket, with bats ranging from tennis rackets to lumps of wood from the demolition site across the road. The usual arguments followed of course. Was it

LBW? Did I hit the ball? Was I caught or did the ball hit the ground first? Extra staff were drafted in to the playground at lunchtimes to control the mayhem and prevent GBH. The boys really wanted to be on the team.

There was quite a large contingent of Afro-Caribbean boys and one in particular stood out from the crowd. He was called Andrew Cole, not the Andy Cole who played for Manchester United, Newcastle, Sunderland, Arsenal and Manchester City etc. Andrew was quite tall for his age, had a huge black Afro cut and a pair of steely blue eyes that showed no emotion whatsoever. His father was Jamaican and his mother was Irish, a feisty combination. He was always in trouble, He was once the subject of a beating by the Headmaster and he stood there and took it, looking straight at the Head with those emotionless blue eyes, never flinching once.

However, Andrew's passion was cricket and whilst he was handy with the bat, he was also a very good fast bowler, his heroes being Wes Hall and Charlie Griffiths, the West Indian demon bowlers. Naturally, he was selected to play along with ten other ragamuffins, four West Indians, one Greek, One Irish, one Pakistani and the rest of English descent. Every available minute was spent in the school playground practising for this first ever cricket competition in the school.

At last, the day of the event arrived. Everyone was turned out well, black trousers, white shirts, clean trainers and even blazers. Some of this had been begged and borrowed. We all piled into the mini bus with Rod at the helm, and we also had a bag of kit containing three sets of pads, two balls, wicket keepers gloves and two bats. The boys were so excited.

We arrived at Carmel. My, it was a posh school, with fantastic buildings, playing fields and even a cricket pavilion with a proper scoreboard. We all piled out of the minibus and were shown the visitors' dressing room, with benches, hooks and lockable lockers. Showers and toilet facilities were also available and were all spotlessly clean. Their staff member was a really nice chap and we tossed a coin to see who had choice of batting. They won and put us in to bat. What was that all about?

Our openers strolled out looking rather dapper in their white shirts with black trousers and pads. Not as dapper as the opposition, however, who were all in cricketing whites and boots, and applauded us onto the batting strip. What was that all about? There were proper Umpires in white coats and one even had a cricket pullover wrapped round his waist. Our boys must have been overawed, but they didn't show it.

The Umpire yelled to our opener,

"What guard do you require?"

"Yer wha'?"

"Leg, middle, middle and leg?"

"Oh yes please," came the reply.

After all the shenanigans were sorted out, he started play. The first few balls produced a couple of singles and then one of our openers was given out. Mumblings of "Never" and "Nowhere near" could be heard as he trudged off the field. Our number three was not known for his finesse. He was a huge Greek lad, whose belly measurement was probably the same as his height. He got to the crease and hammered a couple of fours and a six in quick succession before he was caught on the boundary. Cole came in next and did roughly the same as his predecessor before being given out to LBW. The Umpire got the full steely glare, as Cole trudged back to the pavilion.

Rapid wickets fell and before the twenty overs were up, we were all out for fifty-five, about as much as we expected. Everybody came in and we had orange juice and biscuits before our turn in the field. By this time our boys had got the hang of clapping batsmen in to the crease. But that was where the politeness ended, as we unleashed "The Cole." He marked out his run up of about thirty paces whilst shouts from the pavilion of "That's a little excessive," "I think he fancies himself as a bowler! Ha! Ha!" etc could be heard.

The steely blues were glinting in the afternoon sunshine as Cole started his run up. The venom was there for all to see as he released the ball like an Exocet missile and very nearly took the batsmen's head off. The second ball was more controlled and equally venomous as it flattened all of the stumps. The batsman hadn't a clue! Number three was despatched two balls later and number four quickly followed. The scoreboard looked incredible

Carmel **0** for **3**

As the other bowler took his turn, a few singles were taken and then it was Cole's turn to bowl again. There must have been fear in the batsman's eyes, as the steely blues were advancing like an express train.

Very soon it was all over. Carmel were all out for twenty-two runs and Cole's bowling had humiliated their school. He had bowling figures of eight wickets for six runs and obviously was named 'the man of the match'.

Their teacher and their captain came over to congratulate us, which was very sporting. More importantly, they wanted to know if Cole was a county player, it was all very exciting.

Our next match was against a comprehensive in Aigburth. We lost. Cole was excluded for a week for another misdemeanour and was not allowed to play.

Who said one man doesn't make a team?

Footy was the main sport and even though we did not have our own school field, we could still do practices in the school playground. We used to share playing fields with the University and other schools. In the semi-final of one of the cup matches we played, quite a number of staff and parents actually attended – a rare event at our school. We were away from home and I was put in charge of the team, so we had to discuss tactics before the match. We were lucky to have a very strong and powerful centre forward, so the obvious tactic was to get the ball to the wingers, who were then to advance and put in crosses for our big man down the middle.

All was going well and there were lots of shouting, encouragement and applause from all of the spectators. It was a very close match and we were fortunate to be leading by a single goal with about ten minutes to go before half time. Suddenly, we noticed this one stocky chap in a tracksuit who had appeared on the touchline. He was yelling ferociously and he had a voice like thunder! Every time our player got the ball, there was a tirade of abuse and foul language "Hack him down,"

"Kill the little s***, don't let the ba****d get past you!"

"Have his legs. Don't be a f******g t***, foul him."

This was turning really nasty and so I had a word with the Ref at half time, asking him if he would speak with this chap, as his comments were really abusive.

"Oh, I can't do that. He's our Head of PE."

Nil desperandum.

The end of the year couldn't come soon enough. I had just about survived most of the ordeals that were put in front of me. Uncle John was very gracious and said that he had to complete a report to the local authority stating my progress and competence as a new teacher, and it had been quite favourable. One of my probationary colleagues had had a nervous breakdown in the Easter term and many were amazed he had lasted so long. He was not cut out for teaching in this type of challenging environment and I later heard he had found himself a post at a prep school in Wiltshire, where he had found his feet.

As the final assembly came to a close with three cheers for the teachers, the school gates were opened and the Mongol hordes poured out. The staff retired to the staff room, where the headmaster had laid on nothing – which was to be expected. A few staff who knew the drill had come prepared and there were several bottles of homemade wine on a side table, with a few dozen paper cups. Beside these was a sign, "Please help yourself!" which was a lovely gesture. A couple of the staff played musical instruments and so we spent a happy hour getting very merry on homemade wine and listening to music. At about 5.30pm, the instruments were put away and we adjourned to the local pub on the corner, where we filled the bar at opening time. A kitty was formed in an ashtray and if anyone wanted a drink, they just helped themselves. Some of the staff, who had large appetites for booze, threw in twice the required amount which I thought was decent of them.

As the evening progressed and people were getting more and more jovial, I was called to the bar by the barman. Fearing I had done something untoward (we had all been rather loud and boisterous), I was fearing the worst. As I reached the bar, he thrust a pint of beer towards me and said it was from the lads next door in the lounge. I didn't know anyone in this area, so I peered through the gap and saw three of my fifth year who had just left, all giving me the thumbs up. Wow! I must have done something right.

Chapter 7
Relative Days

The black sheep

A lot of families have someone who they do not wish to talk about. Maybe they brought disgrace to the family in some way. Our family was no exception. We had Uncle Alan.

Uncle Alan didn't change much over the years. He had black, slightly greasy hair, swept back and parted down the middle. A thin, black moustache on his top lip completed his make-up. He was very long and thin, possibly over six feet tall and his clothes seemed to hang off him. He was normally dressed in a scruffy double-breasted dark suit, except when he was 'working'. Now, 'work' was a word that was alien to Uncle Alan, as sometimes he had several 'part-time' jobs that required very little work. No-one at the Dole Office knew about these little extra jobs, as they were either illegal or avoided any kind of taxation or National Insurance. Having said all of that, he was a very kind and warm-hearted man, who was totally family orientated, except when it got in the way of his boozing. He had a phenomenal affinity for alcohol and it was only in his later years that I ever saw him staggeringly drunk.

He could buy (or obtain!) and sell absolutely anything. There were times when he bought (obtained) some item totally unseen as he had a buyer for it. People would go to Uncle Alan when they wanted something and couldn't afford to pay the full price. He had a network of contacts that seemed to supply anything and everything. Most of his habits were obtained from a very early age, as his father died when he was relatively young and he had two brothers who were brought up by his mother (my grandmother). Times were hard and they scraped a reasonable living, mainly due to the exploits of Uncle Alan. He left home and married Margaret when he was in his twenties and so the remaining brothers were forced to work, despite having the necessary acumen for further education.

Alan, on the other hand, continued with his dodgy ways. Two or three very part-time jobs, cash in hand, were very useful when you were on the Dole. All of these jobs served a purpose, in that he met a lot of people with certain needs and wants. He did not deal in drugs, apart from cigarettes and alcohol, which he frequently went across to France for. His main loss of income was in the pub, where he was found most lunchtimes and evenings. How these pastimes were funded remained a mystery to me for many years, until I realised he was running an illegal 'book' and was taking bets from those on his council estate.

This continual alcohol abuse continued all the way through his teens and into his twenties, before he suffered from tuberculosis. After this diagnosis, he was admitted to a 'sanatorium' to recuperate. He asked for a ground floor ward, as he said he did not like heights and he was prone to sleepwalking. Somehow, the nursing staff fell for this and he was placed in a ward with four beds on the ground floor. I'm sure it was with complete amazement that the other occupants watched Alan put his clothes on over his pyjamas after lights out, and disappear out of the window, to return three hours later having spent the time in the pub. His excuse to the rest of the inmates was that the doctor told him he had to drink lots and he was just doing what the doctor ordered! Naturally, the doctor had meant water, and he also forgot to mention about not smoking Woodbines and roll-ups. It was with constant amazement too that the nurses had to empty an overflowing bed pan each morning!

Uncle Alan's favourite drinking pal was his cousin George. George, however, worked as a steward on big ships and was often away for two months at a time.

During his time away, George did not touch a drop of alcohol and worked long hours in order to get more money. Consequently, when he came back, he had two months' pay and overtime money as well. The first thing he would do on reaching home port would be to contact Alan. After spending a short time with his family, George would arrange to meet Alan at the local hostelry at 11am, which was opening time. The two of them would be seen queuing up in their Sunday best at about ten minutes to bewitching hour, ready for the doors to open. Finally, when the doors were flung open by the landlord, the two would rush inside as though they had not had a drink in weeks. In George's case, this was true, but in Alan's case, it was probably hours. The first order went like this, "Bob, George. Are ya aalreet bonnie lads?"

"Canny man,"

"Is it the usual lads?"

"Aye. Twenty pints o' best Jack."

Now this might seem a little excessive to the casual observer, but the beer was pulled from hand pumps and took a little while to pour. The first few pints never touched the sides and they would drink it as soon as it was poured. Consequently, there was never a queue of glasses on the bar. It was only after the barman had poured ten pints that a queue of full glasses began to form. If any of their mates popped in, there was a beer there, already poured, waiting for them. Their appetite for beer was quite phenomenal and the first 'round' only lasted just over the hour. The next round was halved, only the ten pints were ordered. By the time they were pulled, two or three each had been drunk.

Obviously, they couldn't keep up this incredible rate of consumption so there must have been lots of comfort breaks. However, by the time the pub closed at 3pm, they had consumed twenty-five pints each. To the normal mortal, this would result in death by drowning, but to Alan and George, it was just a thirst quencher. No doubt the landlord looked forward to George being at home, as his profits must have doubled.

Staggering out of the pub shortly after 3pm, the two made their way home, as they lived close to each other. A sandwich and a snooze was the order of the day. Wives were given instructions to wake the sleeping beauties at 6pm, when after a quick wash and brush up, they met once again at the pub at 7pm. Now this was late according to their standards, but the evening session could last longer, as the pair knew of various 'clubs' where drinking could take place outside of normal licensing hours. It was also more relaxed and consequently, the order was for four pints at a time. As they moved on from one drinking den to another, the flow gradually eased and Alan then turned to brandy, presumably as he couldn't take any more volume.

This continued for the two weeks (or until George ran out of money) that George was at home. When George was recalled to the ship, he immediately stopped drinking alcohol. Unfortunately, Alan did not.

In England in 1972, the majority of power stations were fuelled by coal which was obtained from the North Eastern, Yorkshire, Nottinghamshire and Welsh coal fields. This was a little unfortunate, as there was a miners strike and the NUM called out all its members. Even though the power stations had large stocks of coal, it was going to run out sometime. After a stand off by the NUM and the Government, negotiations finally started to take place, mainly because the coal stocks were diminishing. Power cuts were in evidence and the public clamour was gaining momentum. The strike lasted about seven or eight weeks and it was particularly noticeable, as it was a very cold start to the year.

Once the strike was over and the miners went back to work, the twenty ton trucks full of coal started to roll towards the power stations. Because demand was so high and stocks were so low or non-existent, they were passing Uncle Alan's house at the rate of one every fifteen minutes. During one of his more sober moments, Uncle Alan had the idea for one of his 'schemes.'

There was a civilian airfield very close to Uncle Alan's house and there was an unused compound which was fenced off with three metre wire fencing and barbed wire on the top. There was nothing in this compound, although it remained locked with a heavy chain and large padlock. Uncle Alan managed to remove this padlock and open the gates. Next he 'borrowed' some traffic cones and a barrier and set these out on the road next to the gate for the airfield. The barrier remained open, so that cars, buses etc. could pass freely. He then 'borrowed' a lantern and a 'noticeable' jacket (the equivalent of a high viz jacket) and positioned himself ready to lower the barrier.

As the first truck appeared, he lowered the barrier and flagged the truck down by waving his lantern. The driver was a little confused, until Uncle Alan explained that there was a very large queue of trucks at the power station and he had been given the authority to get the drivers to dump their coal in the lockable compound, so as not to cause any more traffic problems. This would keep the supply of coal moving and it could be collected at a later date. Strangely enough, the driver agreed and drove into the compound where he dumped his load. This happened with the next five or six trucks, until the compound was filling up. When it was virtually full, he removed the barrier and cones from the road and locked up the compound with the chain and a large brand new padlock.

At the pub that evening, he let it be known that he was selling cars full of coal for a particular price, a fiver. Vans were obviously more expensive and customers had to bring their own sacks and shovels. Because of the strike, coal was in very short supply and about 80% of homes used coal for heat and hot water, so there was bound to be no shortage of customers.

The following morning, as the gates were opened, a steady stream of customers began filling coal sacks and stashing as many as possible in all kinds of cars. A fiver for a car full of coal was a real bargain and there was about a hundred tons of it. Suddenly, after about twenty or so customers, there were a number of blue flashing lights from across the airfield and cars approaching at quite a speed. Without further ado, the queue of cars disappeared rapidly as four police cars got closer. The lead car applied its brakes just in front of Uncle Alan and the policeman sprang out.

"I hear you've been selling coal for a fiver a car full."

"Now who told you that?"

"We have good informants."

"So what happens next?

"Well here's twenty quid and we'll fill up these four cars. Is that alright?"

"Oh yes. I'm always pleased to help officers of the law."

Well the police have to keep warm too.

One branch of the family lived in Sheffield and in the late sixties, the matriarch of the Sheffield contingent passed away. Aunt Flo was a lovely old lady and I remember her with fondness when she came to stay with us whilst my mother and father went on a holiday cruise around the Med. She was a wonderful cook and made the biggest Yorkshire puds I have ever seen, filling them with luscious gravy. She never got flustered or upset, even when I was being a little bugger. I was too young to travel to her funeral in Sheffield, but my mother and father both went. So too did Uncle Alan. Needless to say they had different travel arrangements. On the day of the funeral, my mother and father set off before midday, as the funeral was at 3pm.

Uncle Alan did not have a car. However, he had noticed a car on bricks with two of its wheels off as the owner was doing some repairs. He therefore 'borrowed' two wheels from a car park and fitted them to the car on bricks at the dead of night. Amazingly, the car door was unlocked and somehow he managed to start it after carefully removing the bricks. He drove it away and parked it overnight, as he was going to the funeral the next day. At about 10am the following morning, he set off after blagging some petrol and managed to drive for about an hour before he got thirsty. He stopped at a roadside pub for refreshment, before driving off. He managed another half hour and then had to call in at another pub. This happened all the way to Sheffield city centre, where he stopped in the middle lane of a three lane, one way street to ask directions. He set off again and got totally lost again, whereupon he went the wrong way up a one way street and brought the traffic to a standstill. By this time, a police car had latched on to him and pulled up behind him. The policeman asked what was going on and Uncle Alan told the officer that he was on his way to a funeral and was totally lost. Naturally, this was before the age of breathalysers, or else he would have exploded the thing.

The policeman then proceeded to give him a police escort to Auntie Flo's house and left him at the corner of a cul de sac. Uncle Alan waved goodbye to the policeman and pulled up to the house. As he opened the driver's door, it came off the hinges and he fell out of the car on to the street. Fortunately, he was blind drunk, so he never felt a thing. Some kind person parked the 'doorless' car for him and managed to secure the door.

After the funeral, he arrived back at the house and imbibed a little more of the hard stuff before driving back. What he did with the 'borrowed' car when he got back is anyone's guess. He must have arrived back home safely as we saw him the following weekend.

One of the routines in our family occurred on Saturdays. My mother, father and I used to go into town. Mother would do some shopping and my father would pop into the office, which was open until midday, just to see if everything was OK. I used to rummage round the record shops and occasionally buy something in one of the large department stores. We would all meet up just after midday in the lounge of the Crown Hotel for a swift drink and often a sandwich.

Uncle Alan got to know this routine and frequently popped in to scrounge a drink or three off my father. He was usually in his 'work' clothes, a pair of faded trousers and a long, mucky raincoat.

"Hey up our young 'un."

"Morning Alan!"

"I'm a bit skint. Can you get us a drink?"

"There's a pound. Nip to the bar and get yourself one."

Off he would go to the bar and come back with two bottles of brown ale no change! He would then tip the brown ale bottle vertically upside down into the glass so that the froth miraculously disappeared back into the bottle and the relatively flat beer filled the glass. He put the glass to his lips and the whole pint disappeared down his throat in about five seconds. He then did exactly the same with the second bottle and sat back in his chair, looking around the room.

"Have you got a lawn mower?"

"Yes Alan. Why do you ask?"

"It's just that I've got a pantechnicon outside with two hundred on. If you hadn't got one, you could have had one of them."

"What are you doing with a van full of lawn mowers?"

"I just borrowed it from a lorry park!"

"Alan! Are you mad? You could get arrested for stuff like that."

"Only if I get caught."

"Well, we must go. Use the change to get another beer, if you want one."

We made a hasty retreat. It was obvious my parents were embarrassed by the whole situation. As we went outside, there was a huge lorry parked on double yellow lines at a bus stop. Dad just looked to the heavens, tutted and walked off.

Another routine that was enjoyed by my parents was a nightclub in town. It was more of a cabaret club, with a small restaurant area and casino. They used to get some top class cabaret acts there, including popular singers of the time, comedians, magicians etc. I dropped them off in Dad's car at about 8pm, with instructions to pick them up at around 11.30pm. I then had the car and used to visit friends or just drive about. The roads were fairly quiet and as I had not long passed my test, I used to love going for a drive.

At about 11.15, I would park the car and pop in to the foyer of the nightclub where I would chat to the doormen until my parents arrived. On one occasion, I got there a little early and the doorman told me to put a tie on and go and see the cabaret as it was fantastic. He handed me a tie and I started to put it on as I went upstairs. Horror of horrors! Who was at the top of the stairs? Uncle Alan.

"Hello son. What are you doing here?"

"I've just come to pick up mum and dad."

"I didn't know they were here. I'm just off to the loo. Here, take that cash and put it all on red on the roulette table. I'll be back in a minute."

With that, he thrust a wad of notes into my hand and disappeared to the toilet. I was totally bewildered. I'd never seen so much cash in my life!

I reluctantly made my way to the casino and found the roulette table. I took a few notes and put them on red. The wheel spun round, the ball was added and it stopped on a black number. Thank goodness I didn't put it all on! I put another few notes on red and this time it came up. Uncle Alan still had not returned, so I was feeling quite brave and put half the money on black. To my surprise it came up and I grabbed the winnings, just as Uncle Alan came back holding a very large brandy. He saw how much money I had made, necked the brandy and then told me to go and get him another one (a triple brandy) and gave me some money. I got him the drink and went and found my parents.

"Where have you been?" they asked.

"I got collared by Uncle Alan, who gave me loads of dosh and told me to put it all on red on the roulette table."

"He's a nutcase, that fella. I've told him you will drive him home, if that's OK. Go now, before he has any more drink and before he causes a scene."

Off I went to collect Alan, who was starting to look the worse for wear.

"Come on Uncle Alan! Dad says I'm taking you home."

"Just one more drink," came the reply, "I'm feeling lucky!"

"No Uncle Alan. If you don't come now, Dad wants to go home very soon, so you will have to make your own way."

With that he downed the rest of his brandy and staggered down the stairs. I handed the tie back to the doorman and he laughed when he saw who I was taxiing home.

The journey back to Alan's house was uneventful and I pulled up outside his front door.

"Does your mother have any washing powder?"

"Why do you ask? I think she has plenty."

"Well I've got about fifty boxes of twelve cartons each in the garage. Just thought she might want a box."

"No thanks Alan. I'm sure she has plenty."

With that, he put his hand in his pocket and pulled out a crumpled wad of notes and put them on the dashboard.

"That's the taxi fare!"

"No, I can't take all of that."

"No argument. You're a kind lad and I've got another pocket full."

The car door was opened and I watched him stumble up the drive looking for his front door key. In he went and I drove back to the nightclub to pick up my parents.

When they got in the car, I showed them how much Alan had given me for his taxi fare. There was over £50. It doesn't seem a lot nowadays but back then, I had a holiday job which paid £12 per week for about fifty hours work.

"I can't take that. I'll happily take a quid. Give the rest back to him when he's skint and trying to scrounge money."

"OK son. You've done right!"

And back home we went, a little later than usual

There were many other misdemeanours involving Uncle Alan and his debauched lifestyle. Fortunately, the majority did not involve my family.

As the years progressed, he did not get any better and his drinking was eventually the death of him, literally. His wife, Margaret, who had remained faithful to him for about forty years, divorced him at the age of sixty-five; she couldn't stand it anymore. He spent the remaining five years of his life in a comatose state and died in a Salvation Army Hostel, a desperately sick man. He was a generous man to his family and made sure there was always food on the table whether by legal or illegal means. He managed to father three children. How this happened we do not know, as he never remained sober long enough for relations. How Margaret put up with his antics for so long is also a mystery.

And they talk about the youth of today.